*This book is dedicated to
all the wonderful teachers
around the world who illuminate minds
and inspire hearts, particularly those who possess
a profound love for teaching, and strive to create
classrooms that are not only engaging
but also empowering and
endlessly fascinating.*

A PRACTICAL HANDBOOK ALIGNED WITH
NCF AND **NEP-2020** GUIDELINES

Master the Art of Experiential Learning

Ignite Curiosity, Fuel Critical Thinking, and Transform
Classrooms into Hubs of Real-World Skill-Building

Dr. P.K. Roy, PhD

Foreword by Prof. Dr. Cyriac Thomas

INDIA · SINGAPORE · MALAYSIA

ISBN
Paperback 979-8-89744-955-2
Hardcase 979-8-89929-708-3

CONTENTS

Foreword   *vii*

Preface   *xi*

Introduction   *xv*

Maximizing Your Experience with This Book   *xix*

Chapter 1:   Understanding Experiential Learning   1

Chapter 2:   The Core Elements of Experiential
                     Learning   10

Chapter 3:   Applications of Experiential Learning
                     in the Classroom   17

Chapter 4:   The Importance of Experiential Learning
                     in Today's World   26

Chapter 5:   Experiential Learning and the Skills for
                     the 21st Century   32

Chapter 6:   Experiential Learning Beyond
                     the Classroom   38

Chapter 7:   Challenges in the Implementation of
                     Experiential Learning   45

Chapter 8:   Strategies for Overcoming Challenges
                     in Experiential Learning   51

Chapter 9:   Measuring Success in Experiential Learning   57

Contents

Chapter 10:   The Way Forward - The Future of
               Experiential Learning   65

Chapter 11:   Sample Lesson Plans   75

Conclusion   97

Endnotes   105

May I ask you a little favor?   119

A Special Gift for You!   121

Acknowledgments   123

FOREWORD

Prof. Dr. Cyriac Thomas

Former Vice Chancellor,
Mahatma Gandhi University, Kottayam, &
Head of the Department of Political Science,
St Thomas College, Pala.

Education has become a household term, in almost all conditions in most languages of the world. The wise men of the East and West from early times used this concept to refer to efforts initiated and worked out in the field of learning. Emperors and scholars in the western hemisphere, as well as rulers and sages in the eastern or oriental spheres also were familiar with the depth and scope of 'education'.

As in Athens, Rome, or China, and certainly in India, education has traditionally remained a teacher-centric mechanism and process. In Athens, it was known as 'Plato's School' or 'Aristotle's Academy', and in India, it was revered with the reputed term 'Gurukul' under the stewardship of well-known gurus or masters. The system and style of the learning process were in tune with the methodology propounded by the heads of particular traditions. People from far and near hastened to join such reputed centers of learning in those days.

No education system or 'schema' can remain staid for long. New visions, perspectives, and patterns were discovered and introduced to match the expectations of the times in tune with the changes taking place all around. Schemes and techniques naturally get updated on the basis of the wisdom and suggestions put forward by seasoned scholars and masters here and abroad alike.

Learning skills get reformed, reshaped, and restructured everywhere in line with local, regional, and global adaptations that happen all around. Moral perspectives and taboos give way to modern, materialistic preferences.

A seasonal review of even established values was found not only natural and necessary but even inevitable in the relentless march of time. Even conservative gurus of conventional traditions had to give in to makeup – or to use a current phrase, to 'make in', adjusting to emerging realities. Theories gave way to 'techniques' or 'skills' to make workplaces more comfortable.

The world and life have become highly competitive these days. The pressures of life and work, to use the new term 'profession,' seem to have crossed all barriers, making the Z-Gen professionals labor under awful stress and strain. As an antidote, they make their weekends both physically and mentally as far away from their workplaces, precisely to forget the tensions and pains of their workday world.

The tragedy lies in that the educational process of our times happens to be in no way providing any precautionary measures to equip our youth to confront the harsh realities of life's challenges and consequent lapses and failures to offer appropriate skill development mechanisms in our alternative systemic reforms in the emerging efforts to redesign and restructure our educational edifice.

It is here I realize the significance and relevance of the book **MASTER THE ART OF EXPERIENTIAL LEARNING**, authored by Dr P.K. Roy, a brilliant teacher and outstanding principal of a premier educational institution, besides his credentials as an educational leader and administrator of the first order. Like any right-thinking educator, Dr Roy visualizes the transformation of classrooms into effective grounds for skill development of the promising 'youth brigade' of our times.

It is high time we changed our vision and perspectives about the learning scenario. Indeed, education and learning have come to a crossroads where we are left with no option but to choose the right direction to reach the correct destination.

The very opening lines of the dedication of the book by the author are indeed heartwarming. It reflects, on the one hand, the love he has for his teachers, and on the other, his appreciation of their commitment to their call for this divine vocation. The author's words of dedication also prove and reiterate the saying that '**Good teachers alone can produce good students.**'

I believe the author himself is the best proof for both. And this book remains the best certification for his quality range as a teacher, an authentic author, and a well-acclaimed educational administrator of our times.

Prof. Dr. Cyriac Thomas
Former Vice Chancellor,
Mahatma Gandhi University, Kottayam, &
Head of the Department of Political Science,
St Thomas College, Pala.

PREFACE

Welcome to *"Master the Art of Experiential Learning!"* As we look at the ever-changing demands of today's world, it's clear that education systems need to evolve. In order to equip learners with essential skills for the future, we must move beyond traditional lecture-based methods that often lack engagement. These conventional approaches frequently fall short when it comes to cultivating critical thinking, encouraging problem-solving, and sparking creativity. David A. Kolb, a prominent American educational theorist, is best known for his work on experiential learning, including the development of the Experiential Learning Theory (ELT) and the Kolb Learning Cycle—a framework that emphasizes learning as a continuous process grounded in experience. According to Kolb, experiential learning, which involves active engagement in real-world scenarios, offers a meaningful alternative by fostering skills through direct, and practical involvement.

With over twenty years' experience in education, I have seen the powerful impact of experiential learning in the classroom. This book is a product of my commitment to this field, combining research, hands-on practice, and a deep enthusiasm for teaching methods that make a difference. My aim is to support educators at all levels with practical guidance on effectively incorporating experiential learning strategies into their teaching.

In the following chapters, you'll find a range of practical insights and techniques designed to enrich your teaching approach. We'll explore the core principles of experiential learning, such as designing impactful learning experience, promoting active participation, and evaluating students' progress. These elements together create an enriched learning environment where students feel connected and engaged.

Whether you're an experienced teacher or just starting your journey, this book offers tools to create engaging and practical learning experiences. Picture teaching physics by building model rockets or exploring ecosystems with a classroom garden. Activities like these help students connect what they learn to real life, making it easier to understand. For example, a math lesson on percentages could involve planning a budget for a fictional event. Such activities not only make learning enjoyable but also spark curiosity.

You'll learn how to design activities that bridge theoretical knowledge with practical applications and provoke enthusiasm and deeper interest in your students.

Rather than asking students to memorize facts, try asking questions that encourage them to think critically. For instance, in a history lesson, you might ask, "What if a certain historical event hadn't happened?" This approach helps students analyze ideas, evaluate them, and come up with creative solutions to problems. These skills prepare them to tackle real-world challenges with confidence.

Students also benefit greatly from working together. Assigning group projects, like designing a water filtration system in a science class, teaches them how to communicate and collaborate effectively. They'll learn that teamwork often leads to better outcomes and that shared effort has immense value.

When students have choices in their learning, they take greater ownership and feel more motivated. For instance, you could let them choose a topic for a research project or decide how to present their findings—whether as a video, presentation, or written report. This freedom helps them grow into independent and confident learners who can adapt and solve problems on their own.

Assessing students doesn't always mean giving exams. Instead, you can evaluate their understanding through presentations, projects, or portfolios. For example, after a lesson on entrepreneurship, students could present a mock business plan. These kinds of assessments go beyond testing knowledge and help measure readiness to address real-life situations.

Through experiential learning, we can make classrooms more dynamic, inclusive, and far more effective. This book invites you to collaborate in transforming education with strategies that engage, empower, and enrich your students' experiences.

Happy learning and teaching!

Dr. P.K. Roy, PhD

INTRODUCTION

"Learning is not the product of teaching. Learning is the product of the activity of learners."

– John Holt

The world around us is changing faster than ever, and the way we teach and learn must adapt to keep up. In the past, learning was often about memorizing facts and listening to lectures. But today, having easy access to information is not enough. The real challenge is using that knowledge in real-life situations. This is where experiential learning makes a difference.

Experiential learning is all about doing. It's learning through hands-on activities, solving real problems, and gaining experience. It helps us think critically, become creative, and adapt to new challenges. This book is here to guide teachers, students, and anyone interested in growing personally and professionally through experiential learning (Kolb, 2015).

Whether you are a teacher looking to change your teaching style, a student who wants to learn more deeply, or a professional aiming to grow in your career, this book offers practical advice and ideas to help you succeed.

The Need for Experiential Learning Today

We live in a world that is advancing at lightning speed. New technologies, globalization, and shifts in society are changing the skills needed to succeed. Now, more than ever, we need to develop a wide range of abilities, such as critical thinking, problem-solving, creativity, flexibility, and good communication. These skills can't be fully developed just by sitting in a classroom and listening to lectures (Itin, 1999).

In any classroom, experiential learning can transform the way students engage with their subjects. Imagine a history lesson where students create a mock United Nations debate instead of just reading about world wars. This approach gives them a chance to develop *communication and collaboration skills* while understanding historical events in a deeper way.

Another example could be in an economics class, where students set up a small classroom marketplace. By creating products, deciding prices, and handling transactions, they not only grasp economic concepts but also learn *problem-solving and teamwork*. This hands-on experience brings theory to life, making lessons more memorable.

Experiential learning also promotes *creativity*. For instance, students in an art class might be asked to design murals for their school walls, representing themes like environmental awareness or cultural diversity. This task allows them to think outside the box, develop their artistic skills, and connect their work to real-world issues.

Adaptability is another important skill experiential learning fosters. In a biology class, instead of simply studying ecosystems, students might visit a nearby wetland to observe and record wildlife behavior. Unexpected challenges, like weather changes or spotting rare species, teach them to think on their feet and handle situations calmly.

Engagement and motivation naturally increase when students see the relevance of their lessons. A teacher could encourage English students to write and perform short plays based on novels they're studying. By stepping into the characters' shoes, they gain a deeper understanding of the stories and their themes.

Practical experiences also ***prepare students for the future***. In a computer science class, students might work on developing simple apps that solve everyday problems. This not only boosts their technical knowledge but also gives them a glimpse of what working on real-world projects might feel like.

Experiential learning equips students with the tools they need to navigate a fast-changing world. By bringing lessons to life, it ensures that education is not just about passing exams but more importantly about building skills for lifelong success.

Everyday Examples of Experiential Learning

Experiential learning can be understood through simple everyday examples.

When children **learn to ride a bike**, they don't just rely on instructions or videos. Instead, they practice, fall, and try again until they succeed. This hands-on process helps them develop balance, coordination, and confidence, which they carry with them into other aspects of life.

Cooking a meal is another example. It's not just about following a recipe; it's about adjusting ingredients and solving unexpected problems like overcooking or burning food. This teaches practical skills, creativity, and the ability to think critically under pressure.

Learning a musical instrument also highlights experiential learning. Through regular practice and feedback from mentors, musicians improve over time. This process focuses on developing specific skills through consistent effort and hands-on involvement.

Volunteering in the community offers a meaningful way to learn. It helps individuals build teamwork, communication, and leadership skills while giving back to society. Volunteering also provides insight into social issues and inspires a sense of responsibility in addressing them.

These examples show that experiential learning goes beyond the classroom, equipping learners with life skills applicable in various situations.

This book, *Master the Art of Experiential Learning: A Practical Handbook for Teachers,* is designed and aligned with NCF (National Curriculum Framework) and NEP-2020 guidelines to guide educators in embracing this approach. Through practical tips and real-life examples, it aims to help teachers create impactful educational experiences, preparing learners for future challenges and meaningful contributions to the world.

MAXIMIZING YOUR EXPERIENCE WITH THIS BOOK

To get the best out of this book, I suggest trying the ideas and techniques with your students as you go along. Keep in mind that starting something new, like experiential learning, can take some time to adjust to. Things might not go perfectly at first, and you may feel like giving up, but I encourage you to keep going.

As you explore this new teaching method, your students are also learning a different way to learn, along with the subject matter. While some classes may adapt quickly, it's normal for the first few attempts to feel a bit challenging. But as your students begin to understand the purpose of learning by doing and get used to the new routines, you'll start to see positive results. So, don't let the initial hurdles discourage you — keep trying, and the rewards will follow.

Chapter 1

UNDERSTANDING EXPERIENTIAL LEARNING

---✻---

*"Tell me and I forget, teach me and I may remember,
involve me and I learn."*

– Benjamin Franklin

What is Experiential Learning?

Experiential learning is a teaching approach that emphasizes learning by doing. The idea is that we learn best when we actively engage in experiences rather than only listening or reading. Instead of just taking in information, learners participate in hands-on activities, reflect on what they've done, and then use those insights in real-life situations (Kolb, 1984).

Think about learning to ride a bike. Reading a manual might explain the basics, but it's only by getting on the bike, balancing, pedaling, and practicing that we actually learn to ride. This hands-on approach makes learning faster and more effective (Smith, 2001).

The Development of Experiential Learning

The concept of learning through experience has been around for a long time, but it became a formal educational approach in the 20th century. Thinkers like John Dewey and Kurt Lewin helped shape this idea.

- **John Dewey** believed that education should connect to real-life situations and encourage active participation (Dewey, 1938).

- **Kurt Lewin** introduced the idea of learning through action and reflection, known as action research (Lewin, 1946).

Kolb's Experiential Learning Cycle

David Kolb's model of experiential learning is a helpful guide for understanding how we learn through experiences. It explains learning as a continuous cycle with four important stages, which can be applied effectively in school classrooms (Kolb, Boyatzis, & Mainemelis, 2001).

1. **Concrete Experience**: Learning begins with doing. For example, students might participate in a science experiment, like mixing baking soda and vinegar to observe a reaction. This hands-on activity allows them to engage directly with the subject.

2. **Reflective Observation**: After the activity, students think about what happened. They might discuss questions like, "What did we observe during the experiment?" or "How did we feel when the reaction occurred?" Reflection helps them connect their experience to their understanding.

3. **Abstract Conceptualization**: This step involves analyzing the experience and understanding the "why" behind it. Teachers can explain concepts such as chemical reactions or gas formation, helping students form clear ideas about what they observed.

4. **Active Experimentation**: Finally, students apply their learning to new situations. For instance, they could design their own experiment to test other reactions, using their knowledge to explore further.

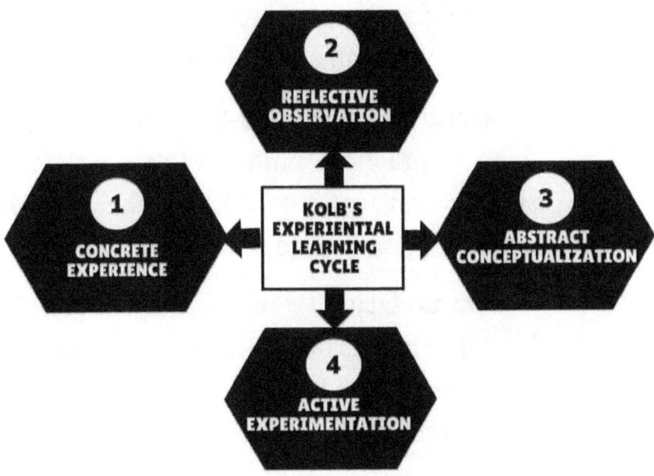

Kolb's model makes learning interactive and meaningful, ensuring students actively engage with lessons while gaining deeper insights. This approach is fun and fosters curiosity!

Kolb's Four Learning Styles

Kolb's learning styles help us understand how students learn in different ways. Each student is unique, and knowing these styles can make teaching more effective (Beard & Wilson, 2013). Let's explore them with examples:

1. **Diverging (Idea Generators)**: These students enjoy thinking creatively and exploring ideas. For instance, during a history lesson, they might enjoy discussing "What if?" scenarios, like imagining how the world

would be different if a famous event had a different outcome.

2. **Assimilating (Conceptual Thinkers):** These learners prefer logic and clear concepts. For example, in a science class, they would love organizing data into charts or diagrams to understand better them.

3. **Converging (Problem-Solvers):** These students focus on practical solutions. In math class, they enjoy solving real-world problems, like calculating how much of paint is needed to cover a wall.

4. **Accommodating (Hands-On Learners):** They learn by doing and experimenting. In a Biology lab, they might learn best by dissecting a flower or building a simple ecosystem model.

Recognizing these styles helps teachers plan lessons that engage all students, ensuring that every child feels included and catered to in his/her learning journey.

Why Choose Experiential Learning?

Experiential learning offers several benefits that make classroom learning more engaging and effective. Let's explore these advantages with examples:

1. **Deeper Understanding:** When students actively participate in activities, they understand concepts better (Hedin, 2010). For example, instead of just reading about photosynthesis, students can observe plants grow under different conditions, making the topic more memorable.

2. **Enhanced Problem-Solving Skills**: Hands-on tasks promote critical and creative thinking. Imagine students designing a water filter in science class—they brainstorm, test ideas, and refine solutions, sharpening their analytical skills.

3. **Increased Confidence**: Practical experiences help students feel more capable. A child who struggles with math can gain confidence by measuring ingredients during a cooking activity, realizing they can apply math in real life.

4. **Higher Motivation**: Interactive learning sparks interest. For instance, a history lesson comes alive when students role-play historical characters, making the subject lively and relatable.

5. **Real-World Preparation**: Applying skills in real-life contexts equips students for life beyond school (Itin, 1999). Think about students managing a mock business—they learn teamwork, budgeting, and leadership, which are valuable in any career.

By connecting lessons to real experiences, teachers can inspire curiosity, build confidence, and prepare students for a dynamic world.

Bringing Experiential Learning into Everyday Life

Learning doesn't stop at the classroom door; it happens in all hours of daily lives too. Imagine the world as a giant classroom where every moment offers a chance to grow and discover. Here's how:

- **Travel**: Visiting new places isn't just fun; it's educational. For example, a trip to a historical site can teach you about past civilizations while experiencing different cultures broadens your perspective.

- **Volunteer**: Helping people makes a big difference, not only for the community but also for yourself. Suppose you join a local clean-up drive; you learn teamwork, leadership, and the value of protecting the environment.

- **Try a New Hobby**: Ever tried baking, painting, or gardening? Picking up a new hobby teaches patience, problem-solving, and creativity. For instance, baking helps you understand measurements and time management.

- **Join Clubs**: Clubs allow you to connect with people who share your interests. A science club, for example, can spark curiosity through experiments, making learning exciting.

- **Face Challenges**: Stepping out of your comfort zone demands courage. Whether it's public speaking or solving a tricky math problem, challenges make you stronger.

These experiences make learning exciting, meaningful, and practical—perfect for a curious mind!

Experiential learning offers a dynamic way to acquire knowledge by actively engaging with the world around us. Unlike traditional methods that rely heavily on passive absorption, this approach places emphasis on doing, reflecting, and applying what we learn in meaningful ways. Through Kolb's Experiential Learning Cycle and insights from thinkers like Dewey and Lewin, we see how structured experiences can transform learning into a powerful tool for personal and professional growth. The hands-on nature of this method fosters critical thinking, adaptability, and confidence while preparing individuals for real-world challenges. Beyond academic settings, experiential learning enriches everyday life through travel, volunteering, hobbies, and other interactive pursuits. By embracing this approach, learners not only deepen their understanding but also develop practical skills that stay with them for a lifetime. Ultimately, experiential learning bridges the gap between theory and practice, making education more relevant, engaging, and transformative.

Key Chapter Takeaways

- **Learning by Doing:** Experiential learning emphasizes active participation in activities rather than passive consumption of information. This hands-on approach leads to deeper understanding and skill development.

- **Kolb's Experiential Learning Cycle:** This model outlines four key stages: Concrete Experience, Reflective Observation, Abstract Conceptualization, and Active Experimentation. By cycling through these stages, learners maximize their learning potential.

- **Diverse Learning Styles:** Kolb's model also identifies four distinct learning styles: Diverging, Assimilating, Converging, and Accommodating. Recognizing these styles can help individuals tailor their learning experiences for optimal outcomes.

- **Real-World Relevance:** Experiential learning connects theoretical knowledge to practical applications, making learning more meaningful and relevant to real-life situations.

- **Enhanced Problem-Solving Skills:** By engaging in hands-on activities and reflecting on the process, learners develop critical thinking, creativity, and problem-solving abilities.

- **Increased Confidence and Motivation:** Active participation and successful experiences boost self-esteem and motivation, fostering a positive learning mindset.

- **Lifelong Learning:** Experiential learning is not confined to formal education; it can be applied throughout life through travel, volunteering, hobbies, and other engaging activities.

- **Historical Roots:** The concept of learning through experience dates back to thinkers like John Dewey and Kurt Lewin, who emphasize the importance of active learning and reflection.

- **Benefits for Individuals and Organizations:** Experiential learning can benefit individuals by fostering personal growth and career development, while also benefiting organizations by improving employee engagement, innovation, and problem-solving.

- **Adaptability and Innovation:** By embracing experiential learning, individuals become more adaptable to change, open to new ideas, and capable of innovative thinking.

Chapter 2

THE CORE ELEMENTS OF EXPERIENTIAL LEARNING

"Experience is the teacher of all things."

– Julius Caesar

Experiential learning means learning through experience. It means getting directly involved, thinking about what we've done, and applying what we've learned in real situations. Here are the main things that make this type of learning work so well: taking part actively, reflecting on our experiences, and always seeking ways to grow.

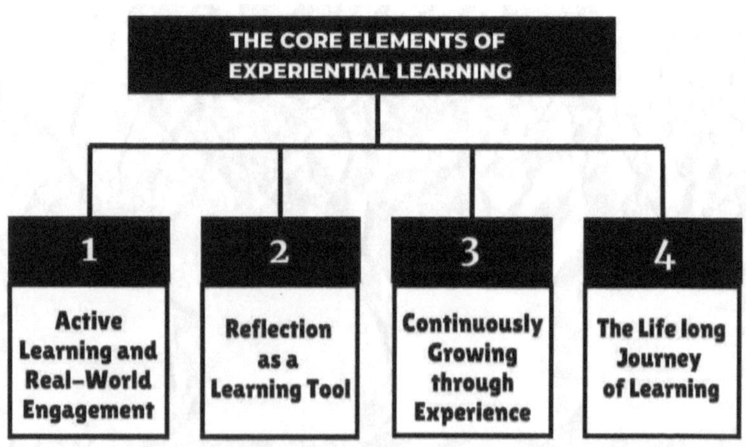

Active Learning and Real-World Engagement

Active learning is at the heart of experiential learning. Instead of just listening to a lecture or reading from a book, active learning encourages learners to get involved (Gentry, 1990). This could mean solving problems, working with others, or doing hands-on activities.

How to Make Learning Active

Active learning makes education exciting and memorable. Here's how you can bring it effectively into classrooms:

1. Use Your Hands:

Learning becomes fun when students use their hands. For example, a student learning about plants could cultivate a small garden, while another studying geometry might build shapes with cardboard. These hands-on tasks make lessons stick to memory because they involve doing, not just listening. Hands-on experience deepens understanding (Beard & Wilson, 2013).

2. Solve Real Problems:

Real-world challenges help students connect learning with life. For instance, instead of just solving math equations, students could budget for a school event or design a simple machine. Imagine an engineering student working on a real design problem or a student helping to organize a community event (Hedin, 2010). This way, they apply knowledge creatively and develop practical skills.

3. Work in Groups:

Teamwork makes learning enjoyable and meaningful. A group can conduct a science experiment or prepare a history presentation together. Sharing ideas sharpens understanding and teaches cooperation. For example, a team preparing for a quiz or a group working together on a science project promotes collaboration and exposes students to different perspectives (Kraft & Kielsmeier, 1995).

4. Explore Beyond the Classroom:

Learning doesn't end at the classroom door. Visiting a local museum, volunteering at a shelter, or observing professionals at work provides insights textbooks can't. For example, a trip to a historical monument can make history lessons come alive (Itin, 1999).

By making learning hands-on, practical, and collaborative, teachers can provoke curiosity and deeper understanding among students.

Why Does Real-World Engagement Work?

Learning through real experiences makes ideas easier to understand and remember. For example, a business student studying market trends gains more by analyzing real-world data, or a medical student learns by watching actual procedures in a clinic. Applying knowledge in real situations helps sharpen skills and keeps students interested.

Reflection as a Learning Tool

Reflection means taking time to think over experiences, notice patterns, and draw out lessons. When students reflect, they are better able to understand both the subject matter and themselves (Dewey, 1938).

Techniques for Reflecting Well

1. **Write it Down**: Journaling helps students remember and process their experiences. It is like maintaining a diary where they can look back on their progress and personal growth (Itin, 1999).

2. **Use Mind Maps**: Organizing thoughts visually lets students make connections and find patterns. For instance, a student might create a diagram showing how ideas in science connect to real-life applications (Schön, 1983).

3. **Talk to Peers**: Discussing with others and getting feedback can bring fresh ideas. This could be like a team debrief after a project or a group discussion in class, where students help each other see things from new angles (Smith, 2016).

4. **Self-Assessment**: Students can evaluate their strengths and weaknesses, identifying areas where they can grow. Self-assessment promotes accountability and helps learners take responsibility for their learning journey (Kolb et al., 2001).

How Reflection Helps Learning

By regularly reflecting, students get a firmer grip on what they have learned. It is like rereading a favorite book—each time you notice something new and better understand the story. Reflection also improves problem-solving since past experiences highlight what works and what doesn't, enabling students to make more informed choices (Lewin, 1946).

Continuously Growing Through Experience

Experiential learning doesn't end with one lesson; it's a cycle that encourages lifelong improvement. Embracing continuous growth allows students to gain more from every experience (Smith, 2001).

How to Keep Improving

1. **Set Clear Goals**: Setting goals gives students direction and motivation. A plan, like a roadmap, helps them stay on track (Kolb, 1984).

2. **Seek Feedback**: Asking for feedback from others brings fresh insights. This is like consulting a mentor or coach who can help guide them toward improvement (Beard & Wilson, 2013).

3. **Take Risks**: Trying new things helps students grow. Whether it is tackling a challenging assignment or taking up a new hobby, stepping out of one's comfort zone is where growth happens (Dewey, 1938).

4. **Learn from Mistakes**: Mistakes are a part of learning. Experiencing setbacks helps build resilience and shows students how to approach challenges from a fresh angle next time (Hedin, 2010).

The Lifelong Journey of Learning

Experiential learning isn't just for the classroom—it's a lifelong journey. By staying curious, trying new things, and regularly reflecting, students can keep learning and growing. It's like setting out on a lifelong adventure, always discovering new things and learning valuable lessons (Smith, 2016).

Experiential learning offers a transformative way to gain knowledge by connecting action, reflection, and real-world application. This chapter delved into its essential components, emphasizing the importance of active participation, thoughtful reflection, and a mindset geared toward growth. Engaging in hands-on activities, tackling real-world problems, and working collaboratively provide learners with practical insights and lasting understanding. Stepping beyond classroom walls to explore real-life settings further strengthens these experiences. Reflection plays a crucial role, helping learners process their actions, identify patterns, and extract meaningful lessons. Techniques like journaling, discussions, and self-assessment foster deeper self-awareness and skill development. By embracing feedback, setting clear goals, and learning from missteps, students unlock their potential for continuous improvement. Experiential learning is more than a teaching method—it's a lifelong approach to personal and professional growth, inspiring learners to stay curious, adapt to change, and embrace challenges as opportunities for development.

Key Chapter Takeaways

- **Active Learning is Key:** Engaging in hands-on activities, problem-solving, and collaborative projects fosters deeper understanding and skill development.

- **Real-World Engagement:** Applying knowledge to real-life situations enhances learning and makes it more relevant and memorable.

- **Reflection is Essential:** Taking time to think about experiences, identify patterns, and draw lessons promotes self-awareness and critical thinking.

- **Diverse Learning Environments:** Exploring different settings, such as field trips and internships, broadens perspectives and enriches learning.

- **Collaborative Learning:** Working with peers fosters teamwork, communication skills, and diverse perspectives.

- **Self-Assessment:** Evaluating personal strengths and weaknesses promotes accountability and guides individual growth.

- **Lifelong Learning:** Experiential learning is a continuous process that encourages curiosity, adaptability, and a growth mindset.

- **Embracing Challenges:** Taking risks and learning from mistakes are crucial for personal and professional development.

- **Setting Goals:** Defining clear objectives provides direction and motivation, promoting progress and achievement.

- **Seeking Feedback:** Actively seeking input from others offers valuable insights and hastens improvement.

Chapter 3

APPLICATIONS OF EXPERIENTIAL LEARNING IN THE CLASSROOM

"What we learn with pleasure, we never forget."

– Alfred Mercier

Experiential learning provides flexible strategies that teachers can utilize to suit students of various ages. By adapting these hands-on methods, teachers make learning more meaningful, interesting, and impactful.

Tailoring Experiential Learning for Different Age Groups

A. Elementary Education

Early childhood is a crucial stage of learning, and adopting engaging methods can make the process enjoyable and impactful for children. Here are three effective approaches:

1. **Play-Based Learning:** Play is a natural way for children to learn and grow. For example, when kids use building blocks, they don't just build towers—they learn to think creatively, solve problems, and work as a team. Imagine a classroom where children collaborate to create a city of blocks, discussing ideas and overcoming challenges together. This kind of play builds essential skills like communication and critical thinking.

2. **Sensory Learning:** Children learn best when their senses are engaged. Activities like playing with sensory bins filled with sand or rice, finger painting, or exploring musical instruments allow them to experience textures, colors, and sounds (Schön, 1983). For instance, painting a rainbow helps children connect colors to real-world phenomena, fostering creativity and sensory development.

3. **Nature-Based Learning:** Outdoor activities spark curiosity and promote exploration. A school garden, for example, is a perfect place for children to observe insects, plant seeds, and watch flowers bloom. Such experiences help them understand the environment and develop a sense of responsibility towards nature.

These methods make learning fun and meaningful, setting a strong foundation for the future.

B. Secondary Education

Learning becomes exciting and meaningful when students connect it with real-world experiences. Here are some effective ways to make learning practical and engaging:

1. **Project-Based Learning:**

   Imagine a class project where students create a sustainable garden. While planning and planting, they learn about science (plant biology), math (measuring garden plots), and environmental studies (reducing carbon footprints). Such projects teach teamwork and problem-solving, making lessons memorable.

2.   **Internships:**

What if students could work with local businesses or professionals? For instance, an internship at a nearby bakery can teach budgeting, customer service, and even chemistry (baking techniques). It's a chance to explore careers while gaining real-world skills.

3.   **Service Learning:**

Helping at a community food bank teaches compassion and responsibility. Students learn about social issues, like hunger, while improving organizational and teamwork skills. These activities also encourage empathy and a sense of purpose.

By incorporating such hands-on experiences into the classroom, students learn not only academic content but also life skills. Teachers can adapt these strategies to suit different age groups, making education a journey of discovery and personal growth.

C. Higher Education

Bringing real-life experiences into the classroom can make learning more engaging and meaningful for students. Let's explore three effective ways to connect learning with life.

1.   **Cooperative Education:**

Imagine students learning about business management in class and then applying these concepts while interning at a local company. This is the essence of cooperative education—combining studies with actual work experience. It helps students understand how theoretical concepts work in real-life settings. For instance, a student studying marketing can work with a business to create a small campaign, gaining practical skills and confidence.

2. **Research Projects:**

Encouraging students to research topics they are passionate about enables them to delve into subjects in depth and develop essential skills, such as critical thinking, problem-solving, and effective communication. For instance, a history student researching the cultural heritage of their hometown not only learns about tradition and identity but also enhances their ability to analyze information and present it effectively. Such projects make learning meaningful and personal.

3. **Study Abroad Programs:**

Participating in exchange programs or study tours exposes students to diverse cultures, education systems, and worldviews. For example, experiencing Japan's unique classroom dynamics and collaborative learning can inspire innovative approaches to teamwork and discipline. These immersive experiences broaden students' perspectives, build their independence, and prepare them to thrive in a globally connected world.

These methods transform learning into an adventure, preparing students for a dynamic, interconnected world.

These methods transform learning into an adventure, preparing students for a dynamic, interconnected world.

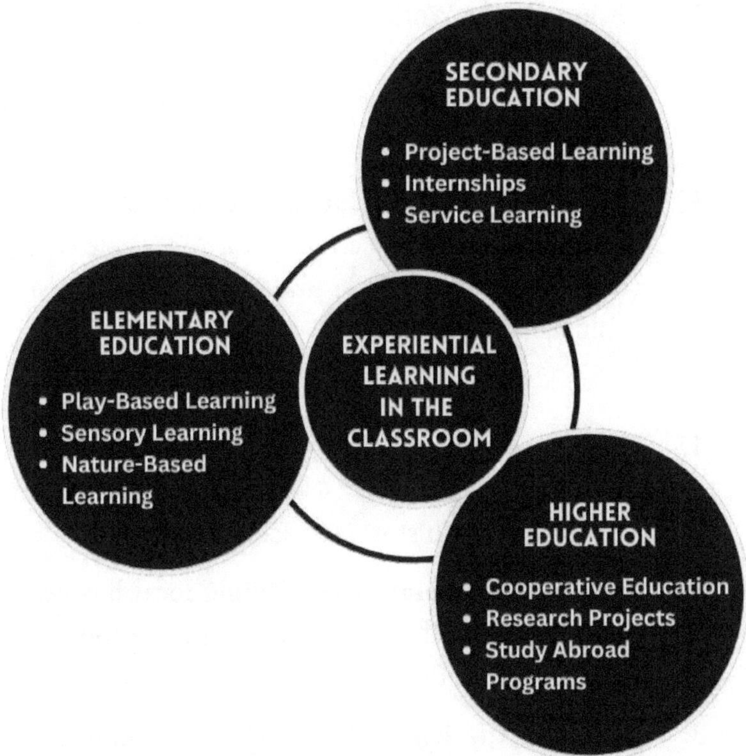

Using Projects, Field Trips, and Simulations for Experiential Learning

Using projects, field trips, and simulations can make learning more engaging and meaningful for students.

Projects

1. **Student-Led Projects:** Letting students come up with and manage their own projects, such as organizing a recycling drive, helps them feel more responsible for their learning.

2. **Group Work:** Working in teams to solve problems teaches valuable teamwork skills. For instance, putting together a class newspaper can build communication and organization abilities.

3. **Real-World Links:** Connecting projects to real issues—like designing a model for renewable energy solutions—helps students understand how their work can make a difference.

Field Trips

1. **Educational Visits:** Going to places like museums or historical sites gives students a direct look into subjects such as history and science.

2. **Community Exploration:** Visiting local businesses or government offices helps students learn about how different parts of society work together.

3. **Cultural Experiences:** Traveling to new communities or countries introduces students to various viewpoints, broadening their understanding of the world.

Simulations

1. **Role-Playing Activities:** By acting out roles in different scenarios, like pretending to be in a courtroom, students get to see complex situations from multiple perspectives.

2. **Business Simulations:** Setting up mock businesses or trading environments lets students practice making decisions and learning about entrepreneurship.

3. **Virtual Reality Experiences:** VR technology can take students to other places or time periods, giving them a deeper understanding of topics like history or science in an interactive, hands-on way.

Fostering Inquiry-Based and Problem-Based Learning

Inquiry-based and problem-based learning methods help students ask questions and get involved in solving problems.

Inquiry-Based Learning

1. **Encouraging Questions:** When students are encouraged to ask questions about different topics, it makes them curious. For example, if a student asks, "Why do seasons change?" It helps them think critically and learn more.

2. **Research Opportunities:** Allowing students to look into their own questions, like studying animals in their area, helps them learn independently.

3. **Exploration:** Giving students the chance to explore what they are interested in, either through individual or group projects, helps them understand better.

Problem-Based Learning

1. **Solving Real Problems:** Giving students real-life challenges, such as finding ways to save water in school, helps them use what they've learned in practical ways (Kolb, et al., 2001).

2. **Collaborative Solutions:** Teaming up to find solutions encourages creativity and teamwork. For

instance, they might create a recycling program for the school (Gentry, 1990).

3. **Reflection and Evaluation:** Thinking about their work and deciding what worked well, such as talking about the results of a project, helps students learn from their experiences (Schön, 1983).

This chapter highlights how experiential learning transforms classrooms into dynamic spaces where students actively engage with their education. By tailoring methods to suit different age groups, educators create opportunities for growth through hands-on activities, real-world connections, and inquiry-based exploration. Early childhood education benefits from sensory play and nature-based experiences, while elementary students thrive with projects and role-playing. Secondary education introduces more complex initiatives like internships and service learning, paving the way for career readiness. In higher education, cooperative programs and global exposure enhance students' perspectives and skills. Strategies like field trips, simulations, and community projects further enrich learning, fostering collaboration and practical problem-solving. By encouraging curiosity and reflection, these approaches prepare students for real-world challenges and inspire a passion for lifelong learning. Teachers who embrace these methods not only educate but empower their students, ensuring a meaningful and impactful educational journey.

Key Chapter Takeaways

- **Tailored Approaches:** Experiential learning can be adapted to suit various age groups, from early childhood to higher education.

- **Meaningful Engagement:** Hands-on activities, projects, and real-world connections make learning more interesting and impactful.

- **Holistic Development:** Experiential learning supports not only cognitive skills but also social, emotional, and physical development.

- **Active Learning:** Students become active participants in their own learning process, rather than passive recipients of information.

- **Real-World Relevance:** Experiential learning connects classroom concepts to real-world situations, making learning more practical and applicable.

- **Skill Development:** Students develop critical thinking, problem-solving, creativity, and collaboration skills through hands-on experiences.

- **Personalized Learning:** Experiential learning allows students to explore their interests and learn at their own pace.

- **Positive Learning Environment:** Engaging activities and collaborative projects foster a positive and supportive learning atmosphere.

- **Lifelong Learning:** Experiential learning cultivates a love for learning and a desire to continue exploring and discovering.

- **Empowered Students:** By taking responsibility for their learning, students become more confident and independent learners.

Chapter 4

THE IMPORTANCE OF EXPERIENTIAL LEARNING IN TODAY'S WORLD

———————— ✖ ————————

"Learning is a treasure that will follow its owner everywhere."

– Chinese Proverb

As the world changes quickly, we need to rethink how we prepare young people for the future. Learning through real experiences is a powerful way to help students not only gain knowledge but also learn how to apply it. This approach, known as experiential learning, is vital in helping students become flexible, skilled individuals ready for a global society. This chapter discusses why this learning style is important today, especially in preparing students for jobs, offering international skills, and using digital technology for virtual experiences.

Preparing Students for a Changing Workforce

Workplaces today are entirely different from the past. Employers now look for people who can think creatively, solve problems, and adjust to new situations. Traditional teaching methods, which often focus on memorizing theory, may not fully prepare students for these needs. Experiential learning bridges this gap by giving students real-life experiences that help them gain practical skills (Kolb, 1984).

For example, imagine a student learning about teamwork in class. Instead of only studying it in a book, they could organize a school event, like a charity drive or a sports day. By planning the event, they learn how to work in a team, solve unexpected problems, and communicate ideas effectively (Kraft & Kielsmeier, 1995). These are the same skills employers value in the workplace such as thinking creatively, solving problems, and adjusting to new situations.

Another example could be students interested in customer service. Instead of just reading case studies, they might spend weekends helping at a local store or café. This direct experience teaches them how to handle complaints, stay calm under pressure, and provide excellent service—all-important for any career (Gentry, 1990).

By learning through such activities, students become better equipped for the challenges of a fast-changing job market. Practical experiences ensure they are ready not just to get jobs but to succeed in them.

Building Global Skills and Understanding

In our interconnected world, it's essential for students to understand different cultures and perspectives. Experiential learning provides opportunities for students to develop global awareness and skills that make them effective in international environments (Hedin, 2010). This approach helps students appreciate diversity and work well with people from various backgrounds.

Take, for instance, students learning a foreign language. Instead of only studying vocabulary and grammar, they could travel to a country where the language is spoken. Experiencing the culture firsthand helps them learn the language better and understand cultural nuances, such as body language and local customs (Itin, 1999). For students who cannot travel, collaborating on projects with students from other countries through online platforms can also help develop these global skills. These interactions teach students how to communicate across cultures and adapt to different perspectives, qualities that are crucial in today's world.

Moreover, when students work on global issues like climate change or public health, they develop a sense of responsibility that goes beyond their local community. For example, a student volunteering with an environmental group learns about sustainability challenges affecting people around the world (Smith, 2001). These hands-on projects encourage students to think about their impact on the world and foster a more inclusive mindset.

Experiential Learning in the Digital Age: Virtual Experiences

The rise of technology has created new opportunities for experiential learning. Virtual experiences enable students to engage in meaningful activities without needing to be physically present (Beard & Wilson, 2013). This is especially valuable in situations where travel may not be possible. Through virtual internships, simulations, and online collaborations, students can gain practical experience and develop important skills from home.

For instance, a student interested in business might take part in a virtual internship with a company in another country. They can attend meetings, contribute to projects, and interact with colleagues online, gaining experience in a business environment. Similarly, medical students can use simulation software to practice diagnosing patients or performing procedures in a safe, controlled setting. This kind of practice not only improves their skills but also builds their confidence before working with real patients (Schön, 1983).

Another exciting example is the use of virtual reality (VR) in education. VR allows students to visit historical sites, explore underwater ecosystems, or even journey through space. In a history class, students can 'walk through' an ancient city and observe details they would typically read about in textbooks. By combining these digital experiences with traditional learning, students gain a more complete understanding and stay engaged in their studies. This approach also helps them become comfortable with technology, a crucial skill in today's job market.

Thus, experiential learning is about more than just gaining knowledge; it builds the skills and mindset needed to navigate a complex world. By preparing students for a rapidly changing job market, fostering a global perspective, and using digital tools to extend learning beyond the classroom, we equip them with the tools they need to succeed. This way of learning helps create individuals who can contribute meaningfully to society, no matter where life takes them.

Key Chapter Takeaways

- **Adaptability for a Changing World:** Experiential learning helps students adapt to the fast-changing world by teaching them practical skills and how to apply theoretical knowledge effectively.

- **Bridging the Skill Gap:** Traditional methods focus on theory, but experiential learning provides hands-on opportunities, bridging the gap between academic knowledge and workplace skills.

- **Teamwork and Problem-Solving:** Activities like organizing events teach students teamwork, problem-solving, and communication—skills highly valued by employers.

- **Practical Customer Service Skills:** Experiences such as working in a café or store teach students to handle complaints, stay calm under pressure, and develop customer service expertise.

- **Developing Global Awareness:** Experiential learning fosters global competencies by encouraging students to understand diverse cultures and perspectives, essential in an interconnected world.

- **Cultural Immersion:** Learning a foreign language through cultural immersion or virtual collaborations enhances language skills and cultural understanding.

- **Global Responsibility:** Hands-on involvement in global issues, like climate change projects, nurtures a sense of responsibility and an inclusive mindset.

- **Leveraging Digital Technology:** Virtual experiences, such as internships or simulations, allow students to gain practical skills without the need for travel, making learning more accessible.

- **Engagement through Virtual Reality (VR):** VR tools offer immersive experiences like visiting historical sites or exploring ecosystems, making learning engaging and multidimensional.

- **Holistic Development:** Experiential learning not only prepares students for careers but also equips them with the mindset and skills to contribute meaningfully to society.

Chapter 5

EXPERIENTIAL LEARNING AND THE SKILLS FOR THE 21ST CENTURY

✖

*"You don't learn to walk by following rules.
You learn by doing, and by falling over."*

– Richard Branson

The landscape of education in the 21st century calls for a new generation of learners. The traditional methods of rote memorization and passive learning have become obsolete. In this dynamic environment, students are required to be flexible, adaptable, and to possess a wide range of skills to effectively navigate the intricacies of contemporary life (Trilling & Fadel, 2009). A key approach that supports this development is experiential learning, which emphasizes engaging students in hands-on experiences and real-world situations as a means of fostering essential skills (Kolb, 1984).

A. Building Critical Thinking, Communication, and Collaboration Skills

At the heart of success in various fields lie critical thinking, communication, and collaboration—three vital competencies (Partnership for 21st Century Skills, 2009). Experiential learning offers numerous opportunities for students to cultivate these skills in a relevant and impactful manner.

Critical Thinking: This learning approach encourages students to challenge existing beliefs, analyze data critically, and assess information rigorously (Facione, 2011). For example, when involved in a science experiment, students may be tasked with interpreting results, drawing conclusions, and providing evidence for their claims. Such activities sharpen their analytical skills and promote independent thought.

Communication: The ability to communicate effectively is crucial for forming relationships, exchanging ideas, and resolving conflicts. Through experiential learning, students can hone their communication abilities by engaging in discussions, presentations, and collaborative projects (Garmston & Wellman, 2016). Students in a debate setting, for instance, learn to express their ideas clearly, listen actively, and respond constructively to opposing views.

Collaboration: Working together towards a shared objective is a hallmark of effective collaboration. Experiential learning nurtures this by prompting students to collaborate on various projects, tackle problems collectively, and exchange knowledge and skills (Johnson & Johnson, 2014). An example of this could be a group of students involved in a community service initiative, where they must allocate responsibilities, coordinate efforts, and support one another.

B. Encouraging Creativity and Innovation

In a rapidly changing world, creativity and innovation are critical for fostering advancement and addressing complex issues. Experiential learning plays a pivotal role in igniting creativity and promoting innovative thinking by allowing students to explore fresh concepts, try out different methods, and think divergently (Robinson, 2011).

Creativity: By engaging in experiential learning, students are encouraged to unleash their creativity and devise original solutions (Craft, 2005). For instance, students in an art class might be tasked with creating a piece based on a specific theme, thereby stimulating their imagination and enhancing their artistic skills.

Innovation: This approach also facilitates innovation by urging students to question conventional practices and generate novel ideas (Sawyer, 2012). For example, when developing a business plan, students may be asked to devise creative marketing strategies for their products, enabling them to think critically and recognize new marketing possibilities.

C. Understanding Emotional Intelligence and Empathy

Emotional intelligence and empathy are fundamental to forming strong relationships, managing conflicts, and making informed decisions (Goleman, 1995). Experiential learning contributes to the development of these competencies by providing students with avenues to engage with others, comprehend emotional nuances, and respond effectively.

Emotional Intelligence: This refers to the capacity to recognize and manage both one's own emotions and those of others (Mayer, Salovey, & Caruso, 2004). Through experiential learning, students get opportunities to reflect on their emotional experiences and those of their peers. For example, participating in role-playing exercises can help students connect with the characters they embody and understand diverse motivations.

Empathy: Empathy involves recognizing and sharing the feelings of others (Davis, 1994). Experiential learning encourages this skill by prompting students to consider different perspectives. For instance, volunteering at a local shelter allows students to connect with individuals in need, fostering a deeper understanding of their struggles.

EXPERIENTIAL LEARNING AND THE SKILLS

Building Critical Thinking, Communication, and Collaboration Skills

Encouraging Creativity and Innovation

Understanding Emotional Intelligence and Empathy

In conclusion, experiential learning serves as a vital mechanism for developing the 21st-century skills necessary for success in today's complex and ever-evolving society. By offering students the chance to participate in practical activities, collaborate with peers, and reflect on their learning, experiential learning enhances critical thinking, communication, collaboration, creativity, innovation, emotional intelligence, and empathy (Dewey, 1938; Bransford, Brown, & Cocking, 2000).

Key Chapter Takeaways

- **Shift from Traditional Learning:** Experiential learning replaces rote memorization with active, hands-on experiences, equipping students to thrive in the dynamic 21st-century world.

- **Fostering Critical Thinking:** Activities like experiments and problem-solving tasks help students analyze data, question assumptions, and think independently.

- **Enhancing Communication Skills:** Engaging in debates, presentations, and discussions allows students to express ideas clearly, listen actively, and respond constructively.

- **Promoting Collaboration:** Group projects and community initiatives teach students to work together, coordinate efforts, and share responsibilities effectively.

- **Encouraging Creativity:** Tasks like art projects or brainstorming sessions inspire students to think outside the box and devise unique solutions.

- **Driving Innovation:** Students develop innovative thinking by questioning traditional methods and exploring fresh ideas, such as devising creative business strategies.

- **Building Emotional Intelligence:** Reflective activities and role-playing exercises help students understand and manage their own emotions and those of others.

- **Nurturing Empathy:** Real-world interactions, like volunteering, encourage students to connect with others' experiences and develop compassion.

- **Preparing for Complex Challenges:** Experiential learning combines practical activities with reflection, helping students adapt to an ever-evolving, interconnected society.

- **Comprehensive Skill Development:** By integrating critical thinking, collaboration, creativity, empathy, and innovation, experiential learning equips students with essential 21st-century skills.

Chapter 6

EXPERIENTIAL LEARNING BEYOND THE CLASSROOM

*"The beautiful thing about learning is that
no one can take it away from you."*

– B.B. King

While traditional classroom education lays an essential groundwork, stepping outside its confines opens up a vast landscape for experiential learning. Engaging with the real world provides learners not only with tangible skills but also with deeper critical thinking abilities and a heightened sense of social responsibility (Kolb, 2015).

A. Community-Based Learning and Civic Engagement

Community-based learning (CBL) connects academic concepts with real-world issues, bringing learners face-to-face with the dynamics of their communities (Eyler & Giles, 1999). This experiential approach enables students to gain insights into their surroundings while fostering positive change and engendering strong local connections.

Key Benefits of Community-Based Learning:

- **Real-World Application**: CBL bridges the gap between theory and practice, applying classroom knowledge to solve concrete issues (Jacoby, 2015).

For instance, a biology student could work on a local environmental project, seeing firsthand how theoretical concepts play out in local ecosystems.

- **Civic Engagement**: CBL encourages students to actively participate in their communities, promoting a sense of responsibility and civic pride (Eyler & Giles, 1999). They are not passive observers but active contributors to social change.

- **Skills Development**: This type of learning environment naturally develops skills such as critical thinking, problem-solving, and teamwork.

- **Personal Growth**: Through CBL, students often discover new aspects of themselves, developing confidence and empathy (Jacoby, 2015).

Examples of Community-Based Learning in Action:

- **Volunteer Work**: Volunteering offers direct engagement with community issues, whether at shelters, food banks, or animal rescues, providing students with a purpose beyond academics.

- **Community Service Projects**: Local clean-ups or organizing events such as charity fundraisers allow students to improve their communities while gaining experience in teamwork and leadership (Billig, 2000).

- **Mentorship Programs**: Students mentoring younger peers develop leadership and communication skills, alongside a sense of accountability.

B. Internships, Apprenticeships, and Work-Based Learning

Internships, apprenticeships, and work-based learning bridge the gap between school and the workforce, allowing students to observe and absorb the nuances of professional environments (Hamilton & Hamilton, 1997). Such experiences offer an invaluable introduction to various career paths, honing job-specific skills and expanding professional networks.

Why Work-Based Learning Matters:

- **Skill Development**: Work-based learning exposes students to essential skills, including technical and interpersonal abilities, along with a better understanding of professional conduct (Dewey, 1938).

- **Career Exploration**: Internships or apprenticeships allow students to test out potential career interests and understand their passions.

- **Networking**: Exposure to seasoned professionals gives students a chance to connect with potential mentors and build lasting professional relationships.

Illustrative Examples of Work-Based Learning:

- **Internships**: These can be short-term or long-term, paid or unpaid, depending on the organization and field. Internships give students valuable insights into industry demands and expectations.

- **Apprenticeships**: By combining practical training with academic instruction, apprenticeships provide a holistic approach to skill development.

- **Cooperative Education**: Students alternate between classroom study and hands-on work, integrating theoretical knowledge with practical experience.

C. Global Exchanges and Service Learning

Global exchanges and service learning offer transformative experiences by exposing students to cultures, challenges, and perspectives outside their usual environment (Bringle & Hatcher, 1996). Such programs cultivate intercultural competence and encourage learners to consider their roles in a global society.

Advantages of Global Exchanges and Service Learning:

- **Cultural Sensitivity**: Exposure to different cultures fosters empathy and a deeper understanding of global diversity (Bringle & Hatcher, 1996).

- **Language Proficiency**: Immersing oneself in a foreign culture accelerates language learning, as students practice in a natural setting.

- **Personal Growth**: Traveling and adapting to new environments allow students to become more resilient and independent.

- **Global Impact**: Service learning initiatives, such as working in education, healthcare, or environmental conservation projects abroad, help students contribute positively to pressing global issues (Eyler & Giles, 1999).

Examples of Global Exchanges and Service Learning Programs:

- **Study Abroad Programs**: These programs let students experience different educational systems, building cultural adaptability and appreciation.

- **Volunteering Abroad**: Programs focused on healthcare, education, and community development offer students a sense of purpose while broadening their worldview.

- **Cultural Exchange Programs**: Living with a host family in a foreign country allows students to gain an immersive experience of another culture in daily life.

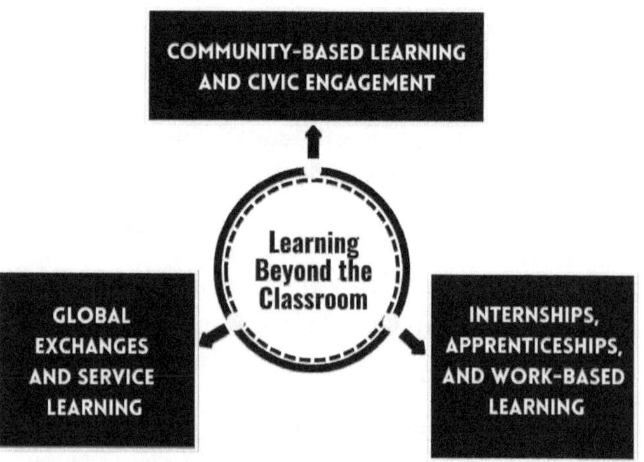

Thus, venturing beyond traditional classroom learning equips students with a well-rounded, hands-on education that builds 21st-century skills and fosters a positive impact on society.

This chapter highlights the transformative power of learning that extends beyond classroom walls. By stepping into real-world settings, students gain experiences that are both deeply personal and broadly impactful. Community-based learning fosters a connection between academic ideas and societal challenges, empowering learners to contribute meaningfully while enhancing their critical thinking and empathy. Internships and apprenticeships provide a glimpse into professional landscapes, equipping students with practical skills and valuable networks. Global exchanges broaden perspectives, encouraging cultural understanding and resilience. Together, these approaches nurture a generation ready to tackle the complexities of the 21st century. Beyond mastering theory, students develop as adaptive, socially conscious individuals capable of introducing change in their communities and beyond. This holistic learning approach underscores the importance of stepping out, engaging fully, and embracing diverse opportunities to prepare for a dynamic and interconnected world.

Key Chapter Takeaways

- **Experiential Learning:** Stepping outside traditional classrooms offers a rich learning experience that complements theoretical knowledge with practical application.

- **Community-Based Learning (CBL):** CBL connects academic concepts to real-world issues, fostering civic engagement, skill development, and personal growth.

- **Work-Based Learning:** Internships, apprenticeships, and work-based learning bridge the gap between education and the workforce, providing valuable skills and career insights.

- **Global Exchanges and Service Learning:** These programs promote cultural understanding, language proficiency, and personal growth while encouraging students to contribute to global issues.

- **Skill Development:** Experiential learning enhances skills like critical thinking, problem-solving, teamwork, communication, and adaptability.

- **Personal Growth:** Engaging with real-world challenges fosters personal growth, including increased confidence, empathy, and resilience.

- **Civic Engagement:** Experiential learning encourages active participation in communities, promoting a sense of responsibility and social change.

- **Career Exploration:** Work-based learning helps students explore potential career paths and make informed decisions.

- **Networking:** Internships and global exchanges provide opportunities to build valuable professional and personal networks.

- **Holistic Education:** A combination of traditional and experiential learning offers a well-rounded education that prepares students for the challenges of the 21st century.

Chapter 7

CHALLENGES IN THE IMPLEMENTATION OF EXPERIENTIAL LEARNING

"The only source of knowledge is experience."

– Albert Einstein

Experiential learning brings students out of the traditional classroom framework, immersing them in practical activities that encourage hands-on understanding and skill-building. While this approach can be transformative, it often comes with certain challenges. Let's delve into three significant areas where experiential learning might hit roadblocks, exploring the reasons behind these issues and potential solutions for educators to consider.

A. Curriculum Constraints and Assessment Limitations

A key obstacle in experiential learning is the rigid structure of traditional curricula, which often prioritizes standardized testing and specific learning objectives over practical, hands-on experiences. John Dewey, a foundational figure in education, emphasized the importance of **_learning by doing,_** arguing that true understanding arises from experience rather than rote memorization (Dewey, 1938). However, today's education system frequently requires educators to adhere to strict syllabi that make experiential activities challenging to incorporate.

Imagine science teachers eager to foster curiosity through a student-led experiment, yet they find that the demands of standardized testing consume most of the available instructional time. The challenge here isn't simply about resources; it's a philosophical clash between two educational goals: covering a mandated curriculum versus nurturing deep, engaged learning. *Traditional assessment methods—such as multiple-choice tests and short-answer quizzes—primarily focus on recalling facts rather than evaluating students' understanding and ability to apply concepts.* According to Kolb's experiential learning theory, genuine learning involves active experimentation and reflective observation, skills not easily measured through conventional assessments (Kolb, 1984).

Educators may find themselves searching for innovative ways to assess experiential learning outcomes. For instance, rather than merely grading a final product, a science teacher could evaluate students' process skills, such as their ability to design experiments, analyze data, and discuss findings. Rubrics can be developed to focus on critical thinking, creativity, and collaboration, aligning more with experiential learning's goals. **'Understanding by Design'**, a work by Wiggins and McTighe, underscores the importance of such assessment strategies, promoting assessments that align with both learning objectives and skill applications (Wiggins & McTighe, 2005).

B. Insufficient Teacher Training and Support

Implementing experiential learning requires teachers to possess both a solid understanding of this approach and the confidence to design meaningful activities. Yet, many educators are not fully trained in experiential teaching methods. This gap in training can leave teachers hesitant as they may feel unprepared to facilitate experiential learning activities or assess students effectively in such contexts.

For instance, a history teacher interested in using role-play to explore historical events might lack the necessary strategies to create a deeply engaging experience for students. Paolo Freire's *'Pedagogy of the Oppressed'* highlights how experiential learning can empower students by putting them at the center of their learning, rather than treating them as passive recipients of information (Freire, 1970). However, without training, even the most dedicated teacher may struggle to bring this vision to life.

Professional development programs that focus on experiential learning can help bridge this gap. Schools should provide workshops where teachers practice designing activities, creating rubrics, and navigating unexpected classroom dynamics. Additionally, teacher training should emphasize collaboration, enabling them to share ideas and troubleshoot challenges together. Linda Darling-Hammond, an educational researcher, stresses the need for supportive professional development environments that empower teachers to innovate and apply new methods (Darling-Hammond, 2006). This can be particularly valuable in schools with limited resources, where teachers might otherwise feel isolated in their efforts to implement experiential learning.

C. Bridging the Gap Between Theory and Practice

Although experiential learning allows students to gain practical skills, a solid foundation in theoretical knowledge remains essential. Many educators have observed that when students jump directly into hands-on tasks without understanding the underlying principles, they may struggle to connect their actions to broader concepts. David Kolb's learning cycle stresses that meaningful learning integrates both concrete experiences and reflective observations, underlining the importance of combining theory with practice (Kolb, 1984).

One approach to balance these elements is the flipped classroom model where students first learn concepts at home through readings or videos, then apply this knowledge through in-class activities. Jonathan Bergmann and Aaron Sams, who pioneered the flipped classroom model, observed that this method enables teachers to spend more time facilitating active learning as class time is freed from traditional lectures (Bergmann & Sams, 2012). For example, a math teacher might assign a video on solving equations for homework, allowing students to engage in problem-solving activities in class. This model has shown promise in helping students understand and apply concepts more effectively, bridging the gap between theoretical understanding and practical application.

In practical terms, this means designing classroom activities that allow students to experiment and explore while continuously drawing connections to theoretical frameworks. A history teacher, for example, could use primary source documents in a role-play setting to help students engage with historical events while also providing context to interpret these sources. This blending of practical engagement and theoretical study can enhance students' learning experiences and deepen their comprehension.

Thus, experiential learning is a journey with its own set of challenges, but by recognizing these hurdles and implementing thoughtful solutions, educators can create an enriching learning environment that prepares students for real-world experiences. Addressing curriculum constraints, supporting teacher training, and balancing theory with practice are essential steps to making experiential learning accessible and impactful. By embracing these strategies, educators can foster a classroom culture that prioritizes engagement, curiosity, and lifelong learning.

Key Chapter Takeaways

- **A Transformative Approach:** The experiential learning method shifts education from traditional lecture-based learning to hands-on, practical experiences.

- **Curriculum Constraints and Assessment Limitations:** Rigid curricula and standardized tests often hinder the implementation of experiential learning.

- **Innovative Assessment Strategies:** Educators can use rubrics and focus on process skills to assess experiential learning effectively.

- **Teacher Training and Support:** Teachers require adequate training to implement experiential learning effectively.

- **Empowering Students:** Experiential learning can empower students by making them active participants in their own learning.

- **Professional Development:** Schools should provide workshops and resources to support teachers in implementing experiential learning.

- **Balancing Theory and Practice:** A strong foundation in theoretical knowledge is crucial for effective experiential learning.

- **Flipped Classroom Model:** This model can help balance theory and practice by shifting some learning outside the classroom.

- **Connecting Theory and Practice:** Activities should be designed to bridge the gap between theoretical knowledge and practical application.

- **Overcoming Challenges:** By addressing curriculum constraints, teacher training, and the balance between theory and practice, educators can successfully implement experiential learning.

Chapter 8

STRATEGIES FOR OVERCOMING CHALLENGES IN EXPERIENTIAL LEARNING

*"Education is not the learning of facts,
but the training of the mind to think."*

– Albert Einstein

Experiential learning offers numerous benefits, but implementing it can be challenging. Here, we look at strategies to overcome these obstacles, aiming to make experiential learning a practical and effective approach to education.

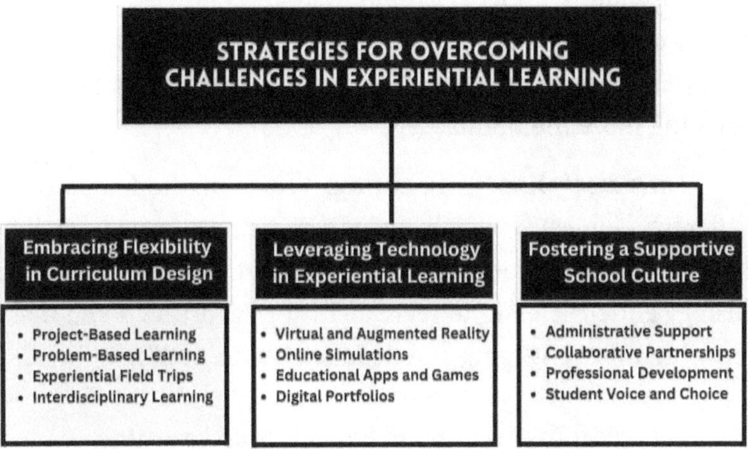

A. Embracing Flexibility in Curriculum Design

One effective way to incorporate experiential learning is by rethinking the curriculum. With some flexibility, educators can create engaging experiences that enhance learning.

Project-Based Learning (PBL): PBL is an engaging way to let students work on projects that relate to real-world applications. For example, a science class might explore solar energy by designing a small solar-powered vehicle. This hands-on experience reinforces learning and has been shown to improve understanding and retention (Thomas, 2000).

Problem-Based Learning: In this approach, students collaborate to tackle complex, real-life problems, which encourages them to think critically and develop teamwork skills. A typical example could be examining a social issue or creating a basic business plan. This method has been shown to deepen learning and enhance student engagement (Barrows & Tamblyn, 1980).

Experiential Field Trips: Going beyond the classroom, field trips allow students to gain firsthand knowledge. Visiting a historical site or a science museum, for example, offers experiences that deepen their understanding and make learning more memorable (Dewey, 1938).

Interdisciplinary Learning: This method combines different subjects, which helps students see connections between ideas. For example, a collaborative project between history and art classes to recreate historical artifacts can make learning more engaging and holistic (Beane, 1997).

B. Leveraging Technology in Experiential Learning

Technology can help create immersive and interactive learning experiences, which are essential for experiential learning.

Virtual and Augmented Reality: These tools let students explore different eras, places, and even skill sets. For example, through virtual reality, students can walk through ancient civilizations, or with augmented reality, they can practice medical techniques. Such technologies provide in-depth learning without leaving the classroom (Pantelidis, 2009).

Online Simulations: Simulations are a fantastic way for students to experiment and understand real-world scenarios, especially in subjects like Physics and Biology where physical experimentation may be limited (Bredderman, 1982).

Educational Apps and Games: Apps make learning interactive. Language learning apps, for instance, provide practice opportunities, while math games build problem-solving skills in an enjoyable way (Papastergiou, 2009).

Digital Portfolios: Students can use digital portfolios to document and reflect on their growth, encouraging ownership over their learning journey and developing critical thinking (Barrett, 2000).

C. Fostering a Supportive School Culture

Creating a supportive culture for experiential learning is crucial to its success. Here's how:

Administrative Support: School administrators are instrumental in promoting experiential learning by ensuring that teachers have the resources, time, and encouragement to innovate in their classrooms (Fullan, 1993).

Collaborative Partnerships: Partnering with community organizations and businesses opens up authentic learning experiences. Such collaborations enrich the learning environment and provide students with exposure to real-world challenges (Epstein, 2001).

Professional Development: Regular training equips teachers with the skills needed to implement experiential learning effectively, ensuring students receive quality experiences (Darling-Hammond, 2006).

Student Voice and Choice: When students have a say in their learning, they tend to be more engaged and motivated. Offering choices and letting students participate in decision-making can personalize their education and make it more meaningful (Toshalis & Nakkula, 2012).

Implementing these strategies can help educators bring experiential learning to life in classrooms, transforming students into active, engaged, and capable lifelong learners.

Overcoming the challenges of experiential learning requires thoughtful strategies that transform obstacles into opportunities for meaningful education. By adopting flexible curriculum designs, educators can integrate hands-on approaches like project-based and problem-based learning, fostering critical thinking and collaboration. Experiential field trips and interdisciplinary projects further enrich the learning experience, making knowledge more tangible and relevant. Harnessing technology, through tools like virtual reality, online simulations, and educational apps, adds depth and interactivity to learning, bridging gaps that traditional methods may ignore. Equally vital is cultivating a supportive school environment—administrative backing, community partnerships, and professional development empower teachers to innovate effectively. Encouraging student voice and choice personalizes learning, boosting engagement and ownership. These strategies not only address challenges but also create a dynamic and inclusive educational landscape, preparing students to thrive in an interconnected world.

Key Chapter Takeaways

- **Flexible Curriculum Design:** Rethink the curriculum to incorporate project-based, problem-based, and interdisciplinary learning, aligning with real-world applications.

- **Leverage Technology:** Utilize virtual and augmented reality, online simulations, educational apps, and digital portfolios to create immersive and interactive learning experiences.

- **Foster a Supportive School Culture:** Cultivate a supportive environment through administrative support, collaborative partnerships, professional development, and student voice and choice.

- **Real-World Connections:** Connect classroom learning to real-world experiences through field trips, community partnerships, and industry collaborations.

- **Student-Centered Learning:** Empower students to take responsibility for their learning by providing choices and opportunities for self-directed exploration.

- **Collaborative Learning:** Encourage teamwork and peer learning through group projects and collaborative problem-solving.

- **Critical Thinking and Problem-Solving:** Develop students' critical thinking skills by presenting them with complex problems and challenges to solve.

- **Digital Literacy:** Equip students with the digital skills necessary to navigate and utilize technology effectively.

- **Authentic Assessment:** Use authentic assessments that measure students' skills and knowledge in real-world contexts.

- **Continuous Reflection and Improvement:** Regularly evaluate the effectiveness of experiential learning strategies and make adjustments as needed.

Chapter 9

MEASURING SUCCESS IN EXPERIENTIAL LEARNING

"The great aim of education is not knowledge but action."

– Herbert Spencer

Evaluating student progress in experiential learning is not always straightforward. Unlike traditional learning methods that lend themselves to standard tests, experiential learning involves hands-on, interactive projects that develop a range of practical skills and critical thinking abilities, which are harder to measure with a standard test alone. This chapter explores creative assessment methods and effective feedback mechanisms that educators can use to gauge the effectiveness of experiential learning initiatives. These techniques aim to ensure that the outcomes of experiential education are captured accurately, providing valuable insights for both students and teachers.

A. Assessment Techniques

Assessing student learning in an experiential setting requires diverse assessment strategies that extend beyond the confines of multiple-choice tests and traditional written exams. Here are some effective assessment methods:

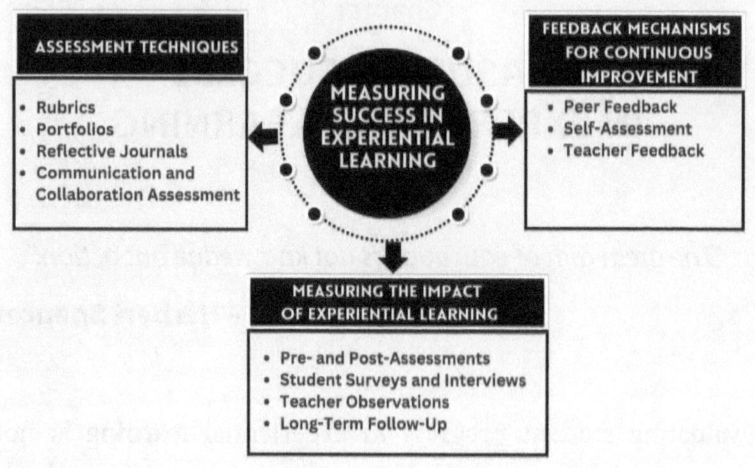

Rubrics

Rubrics offer structured guidelines that clearly outline what is expected of students in experiential tasks, such as projects or presentations. By providing specific criteria for grading, rubrics enable both students and educators to have a shared understanding of the learning objectives and performance expectations (Andrade, 2000). For example, in a science project where students conduct an experiment, a rubric can assess aspects such as their research depth, data collection accuracy, analysis thoroughness, and conclusion validity. This clarity not only strengthens fair evaluation but also empowers students to identify areas where they need to improve.

Portfolios

Portfolios serve as a comprehensive showcase of a student's work over a period of time, encapsulating a range of artifacts like written assignments, artwork, and digital projects. Portfolios allow students to reflect on their progress and demonstrate their learning journey, which fosters critical thinking and self-assessment skills (Paulson, Paulson, & Meyer, 1991). Through portfolios, educators can see growth trends, detect areas of mastery, and identify parts of the curriculum that may call for reinforcement. A student's portfolio in an art class, for instance, might include sketches, final pieces, and reflective statements, each of which illustrates the progression of his/her skill development and creativity.

Reflective Journals

Reflective journals, which encourage students to document their learning experiences and thought processes, are especially effective in experiential learning settings. By regularly writing about their experiences, students deepen their understanding of the concepts and skills they acquire. Reflective journaling not only promotes self-awareness but also allows students to connect theoretical concepts with practical applications thus enhancing retention (Boud, Keogh, & Walker, 1985). For instance, a student in a leadership class might use a journal to reflect on challenges encountered in group projects and how these experiences contribute to personal growth in teamwork and leadership.

Communication and Collaboration Assessment

In a world where communication and collaboration are highly valued, these skills need to be evaluated as part of the learning process (Trilling & Fadel, 2009). Observing students' interactions in group work, presentations, and discussions can reveal much about their development in these areas. Educators may assess these skills by noting how students articulate their ideas, work within a team, and contribute to discussions.

For instance, during a group science project, a teacher might evaluate each student's contribution to the team's objectives, along with their ability to listen, respond, and build on others' ideas.

B. Feedback Mechanisms for Continuous Improvement

Feedback plays a central role in experiential learning as it helps students identify both their strengths and areas for improvement. Effective feedback is timely, constructive, and actionable, guiding students in refining their skills and approaches.

Peer Feedback

When students provide feedback to their peers, they are given an opportunity to engage critically with others' work. Peer feedback promotes empathy, communication skills, and critical thinking, as students must thoughtfully assess another's work and articulate constructive comments (Topping, 1998). For example, in a writing course, students may exchange essays and provide feedback on clarity, structure, and argument strength. This reciprocal process enriches the learning experience by broadening each student's perspective on their work.

Self-Assessment

Self-assessment is an empowering strategy that enables students to reflect on their progress and take responsibility for their learning. By evaluating their own work, students develop critical thinking and self-regulation skills that contribute to lifelong learning (Boud, 1995). For instance, after completing a presentation, students might assess their public speaking skills, identifying areas where they excelled and aspects that could benefit from further practice. This self-awareness helps students set realistic goals for improvement.

Teacher Feedback

Teacher feedback, when provided in a specific, supportive manner, is a powerful tool for fostering growth. It is most effective when it balances the recognition of strengths with constructive suggestions for improvement (Hattie & Timperley, 2007). For example, a teacher might provide feedback on a group project by highlighting effective teamwork while also offering tips for enhancing project management skills. This type of feedback not only validates students' efforts but also motivates them to strive for excellence.

C. Measuring the Impact of Experiential Learning

To gain a comprehensive understanding of experiential learning's impact, it is important to analyze both quantitative and qualitative data. While test scores and grades can offer a snapshot of student achievement, qualitative insights like reflections, interviews, and observations capture the depth and nuances of students' learning experiences.

Pre- and Post-Assessments

Administering assessments before and after an experiential activity allows educators to measure growth in specific skill areas, comparing initial knowledge levels to those achieved post-activity (Black & Wiliam, 1998). For example, in a history class where students participate in a reenactment, pre-assessments might gauge their basic understanding of the historical context, while post-assessments can measure their grasp of details and interpretative skills.

Student Surveys and Interviews

Student surveys and interviews provide valuable insights into how experiential learning influences their understanding, engagement, and attitudes (Flick, 2018). Surveys allow students to express their perceptions of the learning process, highlight aspects they found challenging or rewarding, and suggest improvements. This feedback can be invaluable for refining future experiential learning activities. An interview with students might reveal, for instance, that they felt more engaged with the material because of its real-world application, thereby supporting the continued use of hands-on learning techniques.

Teacher Observations

Teachers' observations are essential for understanding how students interact with the learning material and with one another during experiential activities (Danielson, 2007). Observing students during a role-playing activity, for example, can provide insights into their enthusiasm, engagement, and the depth of their understanding. Such observations allow teachers to make real-time adjustments, providing additional guidance or altering activities as needed to maximize learning outcomes.

Long-Term Follow-Up

Monitoring student outcomes after they leave the learning environment offers valuable information about the long-term impact of experiential learning (Kolb, 1984). Tracking former students' professional achievements, continued education, or personal growth can demonstrate how experiential learning shapes individuals well beyond the classroom. For instance, students who engaged in hands-on science projects in high school may pursue careers in STEM fields, illustrating the enduring influence of experiential learning.

Experiential learning, with its emphasis on active participation and real-world applications, equips students with the skills they need for both personal and professional success. By employing diverse assessment techniques and providing meaningful feedback, educators can accurately measure the impact of experiential learning on students. This approach not only validates students' achievements but also offers a roadmap for continuous improvement, enabling educators to refine their methods and ultimately enhance the learning experience for future students.

Thus, experiential learning's benefits extend far beyond traditional education metrics. Through innovative assessment strategies and targeted feedback, educators can foster an environment where students are encouraged to think critically, collaborate effectively, and approach challenges with confidence. By measuring experiential learning's success in this holistic manner, schools can prepare students to thrive in a complex, dynamic world.

Key Chapter Takeaways

- **Experiential Learning Assessment Challenges:** Unlike traditional methods, assessing experiential learning is complex due to its hands-on nature and focus on soft skills.

- **Diverse Assessment Techniques:** A range of methods, including rubrics, portfolios, reflective journals, and communication/collaboration assessments, can be used to evaluate experiential learning.

- **Rubrics for Clarity:** Rubrics provide clear expectations, aiding both students and educators in understanding performance standards.

- **Portfolios for Progress:** Portfolios showcase student growth over time, fostering self-reflection and critical thinking.

- **Reflective Journals for Deep Learning:** Journals encourage students to connect theory with practice, enhancing understanding and retention.

- **Communication and Collaboration Assessment:** Observing student interactions in group work and discussions reveals their development in these essential skills.

- **Peer Feedback for Growth:** Peer feedback promotes empathy, communication, and critical thinking.

- **Self-Assessment for Empowerment:** Self-assessment empowers students to assume responsibility for their learning and set goals for improvement.

- **Teacher Feedback for Guidance:** Timely, constructive teacher feedback guides students' development and motivates them to excel.

- **Measuring Long-Term Impact:** Analyzing both quantitative and qualitative data, including pre/post-assessments, surveys, interviews, observations, and long-term follow-ups, provides a comprehensive understanding of experiential learning's impact.

Chapter 10

THE WAY FORWARD - THE FUTURE OF EXPERIENTIAL LEARNING

"The best way to predict your future is to create it."

– Abraham Lincoln

Looking to the future, experiential learning stands out as an approach with immense potential to transform education. By embracing the latest trends and adopting innovative teaching methods, educators can work towards creating learning environments that are not only engaging but also equitable and effective. This chapter will explore global trends in experiential learning, outline ways educators can lead change, and discuss how reimagining the traditional classroom can pave the way for a new era in education.

A. Emerging Global Trends in Experiential Learning

Education is evolving globally, and experiential learning is a major force in this transformation. Key trends currently shaping experiential learning include:

- **Gamification**: By adding game-like elements to educational activities, learning can become more enjoyable and compelling. Gamification strategies, such as using point systems, achievements, or progress tracking, have shown to encourage student engagement. Language-learning platforms often integrate these techniques, which help learners stay motivated and make language acquisition less intimidating (Kapp, 2012). In practice, using games to practice math concepts or vocabulary terms can transform a routine lesson into an immersive experience, capturing students' attention in ways traditional methods might not.

- **Virtual and Augmented Reality**: Technologies such as virtual reality (VR) and augmented reality (AR) offer students experiences that would otherwise be impossible. VR can "transport" students to different historical periods, geographical locations, or even scientific environments, giving them a more profound sense of immersion in their learning. Research shows that VR-based learning can enhance students' retention and understanding by allowing them to interact with the material in a hands-on way (Merchant et al., 2014). For example, a biology class using VR might let students 'explore' the human body, providing a memorable and impactful experience beyond textbook images. Augmented Reality (AR) is a technology that overlays digital content (such as images, sounds, and 3D objects) onto the real world in real-time. Unlike Virtual Reality (VR), which creates a completely virtual environment, AR enhances the real-world environment by adding interactive digital elements. AR is typically experienced through devices like: Smartphones & Tablets (e.g., Google map, Snapchat filters), AR Glasses & Headsets (e.g., Microsoft HoloLens, Magic Leap), Heads-Up Displays

(HUDs) (used in cars and aviation). For example, *Medical Training*: AR helps medical students practice surgeries in a simulated environment. *Historical & Science Education*: Apps like Google Expeditions bring historical sites and science concepts to life

- **Personalized Learning**: Tailoring education to meet each student's individual learning needs and interests is increasingly recognized as beneficial for motivation and outcomes. In personalized experiential learning, students often have the flexibility to choose topics or projects they are passionate about, leading to greater engagement (Grant, 2014). For instance, in a project-based learning environment, a student interested in environmental science might research local biodiversity, fostering a stronger connection to the subject matter.

- **STEM Focus**: In the realm of Science, Technology, Engineering, and Mathematics (STEM), experiential learning is vital for connecting theory to practice. With the global push toward developing technological proficiency, many STEM programs integrate robotics, engineering challenges, or coding projects to let students apply what they've learned in real-world scenarios (Honey et al., 2014). Activities like designing a simple machine in a physics class or creating a program in a computer science course give students opportunities to apply theoretical concepts practically.

- **Global Citizenship**: As interconnectedness increases globally, cultivating global citizenship is becoming a priority. Experiential learning can play a significant role here, exposing students to diverse cultures, social issues, and global perspectives. Methods such as service-learning projects, international collaborations, and virtual cultural exchanges allow students to develop empathy, intercultural competence, and a commitment to social justice (Levy & Fox, 2015). For instance, participating in an international exchange program or collaborating on a service project can provide students with a better understanding of issues beyond their immediate communities.

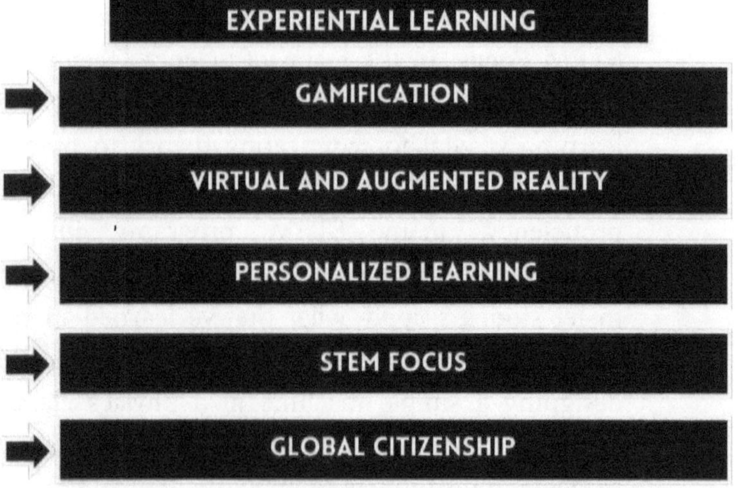

B. How Educators Can Lead the Change

Educators have a pivotal role in advancing experiential learning. To realize its full potential, they must embrace strategies that foster innovation and change:

- **Adopt a Growth Mindset**: Adopting a growth mindset—a belief in the potential for improvement and growth—is crucial for educators looking to implement experiential learning (Dweck, 2006). This mindset allows educators to approach new teaching strategies with flexibility and openness. By modeling a growth mindset, teachers can inspire students to embrace challenges and view mistakes as learning opportunities.

- **Collaborate with Peers**: Collaboration is instrumental in staying current with educational trends and finding support in overcoming challenges. By exchanging ideas, resources, and insights, teachers can help one another adapt and enhance their experiential learning approaches (Hattie, 2015). For instance, a group of science teachers might work together to design an interdisciplinary project combining biology and environmental science, allowing students to see connections across subjects.

- **Engage in Professional Development**: Continual learning is key for educators aiming to refine their experiential learning skills. Workshops, conferences, and online courses can provide invaluable training, exposing teachers to innovative practices and effective assessment strategies (Guskey, 2000). For example, a math teacher attending a workshop on project-based learning might gain new ideas for hands-on geometry activities that help students visualize concepts better.

- **Build Community Partnerships**: Establishing relationships with community organizations, businesses, or local universities can open doors to real-world learning experiences. These partnerships often enable students to engage in meaningful projects that foster a sense of purpose and responsibility (Higgins et al., 2011). For example, a school partnering with a local environmental agency might give students the opportunity to participate in fieldwork or conservation efforts, providing real-world applications for environmental science lessons.

- **Advocate for Experiential Learning**: Educators can support experiential learning by advocating for it at various levels, including school boards, districts, and even state-level education policy. By highlighting its benefits and sharing success stories, teachers can influence policy and funding to support experiential education (Fullan, 2007). Advocacy might involve presenting experiential learning outcomes to school administrators or parents to demonstrate its impact on student engagement and achievement.

HOW EDUCATORS CAN LEAD THE CHANGE

- ADOPT A GROWTH MINDSET
- COLLABORATE WITH PEERS
- ENGAGE IN PROFESSIONAL DEVELOPMENT
- BUILD COMMUNITY PARTNERSHIPS
- ADVOCATE FOR EXPERIENTIAL LEARNING

C. Reimagining Education Through Experience

To meet the demands of the modern world, education must evolve beyond traditional models. Experiential learning allows for a reimagination of the classroom and curriculum, fostering practical skills and critical thinking that prepare students for real-world challenges.

- **Flexible Learning Environments**: Traditional classrooms can be limiting. By redesigning classrooms into flexible learning spaces, educators can create environments that support various activities such as group projects, presentations, and hands-on experiments. Such spaces encourage collaborative learning and active participation, facilitating experiential learning (Oblinger, 2006). For example, a history classroom might have areas set up for role-playing historical events, enabling students to "step into" the past.

- **Student-Centered Learning**: In experiential education, students are often encouraged to take responsibility for their learning. A student-centered approach allows them to choose projects and explore topics of interest, fostering intrinsic motivation and engagement (Weimer, 2013). For instance, in a student-centered English class, learners might choose to create presentations on themes that resonate personally, promoting deeper engagement with the material.

- **Authentic Assessment**: Traditional assessments like exams may not fully capture a student's understanding or skills. Instead, authentic assessment methods such as portfolios, project presentations, and peer reviews provide a more comprehensive picture of a student's learning journey (Mueller, 2005). An art class, for example, might require of students to compile a portfolio of their work and explain their creative process rather than taking a written test.

- **Fostering Lifelong Learning**: A fundamental goal of experiential learning is to instill a love of learning that persists beyond formal education. By encouraging students to pursue topics they're passionate about, educators can help them develop skills for self-directed learning, equipping them to continue exploring, questioning, and growing throughout life (Mezirow, 1997). For example, a science fair project might spark a lifelong interest in Biology or Environmental studies, guiding students toward a career in these fields.

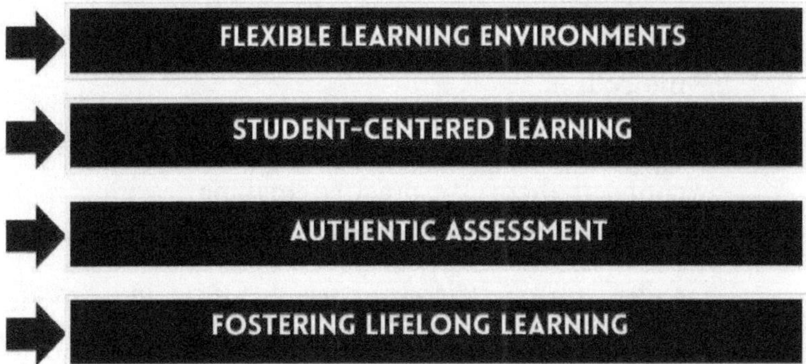

The potential for experiential learning to reshape education is vast. By embracing global trends, committing to ongoing learning, and reimagining the classroom, educators can create meaningful and transformative experiences for students. As experiential learning becomes more widely adopted, it is poised to prepare students not only for academic success but also for the real-world demands of the 21st century.

Key Chapter Takeaways

- **Experiential Learning as a Transformative Force:** This approach is reshaping education globally, making learning more engaging, effective, and equitable.

- **Emerging Trends in Experiential Learning:** Key trends include gamification, VR/AR, personalized learning, STEM focus, and global citizenship.

- **The Role of Gamification:** By incorporating game-like elements, educators can enhance student motivation and engagement.

- **The Power of VR/AR:** These technologies provide immersive learning experiences, transporting students to different times and places.

- **Personalized Learning:** Tailoring education to individual needs fosters deeper understanding and motivation.

- **STEM Focus:** Experiential learning in STEM fields connects theory to practice, making learning more relevant.

- **Cultivating Global Citizenship:** Experiential learning can expose students to diverse cultures and social issues, promoting empathy and intercultural competence.

- **Educators as Leaders of Change:** By adopting a growth mindset, collaborating with peers, engaging in professional development, building community partnerships, and advocating for experiential learning, educators can drive this transformation.

- **Reimagining the Classroom:** Creating flexible learning environments, adopting student-centered approaches, using authentic assessments, and fostering lifelong learning are essential for effective experiential education.

- **Preparing Students for the Future:** Experiential learning equips students with the skills and knowledge needed to thrive in the 21st century, making them adaptable, creative, and critical thinkers.

Chapter 11

SAMPLE LESSON PLANS

"What we have to learn to do, we learn by doing."

– Aristotle

Experiential learning is all about learning by doing. Instead of just listening to a teacher or reading from a book, students get to dive into activities that help them understand the material better. They get to try things out, think about what they've learned, and see how it works in real life. This way of learning makes the lessons more interesting and helps students remember what they learn for longer. Students develop important skills like critical thinking, creativity, and a deeper understanding of a subject by participating in activities like group work, hands-on experiments, and discussions.

In many traditional classrooms, learning mostly happens through lectures and textbooks. But with experiential learning, students become active participants in their education. They connect what they learn to the real world through activities like group projects, field trips, role-playing, and simulations. For example, instead of just memorizing facts about photosynthesis, students can actually observe the process through experiments, which helps them understand it more clearly.

This method works well because it addresses different learning styles. Students aren't just sitting back and listening—they're learning by doing, thinking about their experiences, and sharing their thoughts with others. It also helps them develop important life skills like teamwork, communication, and problem-solving, all of which are useful in school and later in their careers.

In the next few pages, you'll find lesson plans for subjects like Social Science, English, Mathematics, and Science. These plans show how you can use experiential learning in different subjects, helping students not just understand the theory but also apply what they've learned in everyday situations

Social Science

Lesson Plan: Teaching Social Science through Experiential Learning

Topic: *Understanding Community and Civic Responsibility*

Grade Level: High School

Duration: 60 Minutes

Objective

By the end of the lesson, students will:

1. Understand the concept of community and the importance of civic responsibility.

2. Relate their daily actions to the larger impact on their community.

3. Apply the principles of civic responsibility through a practical activity.

Materials Needed

- Chart papers and markers
- Sticky notes
- A set of printed "community scenarios"
- A whiteboard and markers

Lesson Outline
1. Introduction (10 Minutes)

Objective: Arouse curiosity and connect the topic to students' lives.

1. Start with a question: *"What does community mean to you?"*

    - Encourage students to share examples from their own neighborhoods, schools, or places they visit.

    - Write their responses on the board.

2. Introduce the idea of civic responsibility by asking: *"How do your actions affect others in your community?"*

    - Highlight relatable examples: recycling, helping a neighbor, or following traffic rules.

Transition to Activity: Explain that today's lesson will involve real-life problem-solving to learn about being responsible members of a community.

2. Experiential Activity (30 Minutes)

Objective: Engage students in hands-on learning to explore civic responsibility.

Step 1: Group Formation (5 Minutes)

- Divide the class into small groups of 4–5 students each.

- Distribute chart paper, markers, and a set of 'community scenarios' to each group.

Step 2: Activity Instructions (5 Minutes)

- Each group will read a scenario that describes a community problem (e.g., littering in the park, lack of clean water, or bullying at school).

- Their task:
    - Identify the issue.
    - Discuss the possible impact on individuals and the community.
    - Suggest practical solutions they can implement as students.

Step 3: Group Work (20 Minutes)

- Students collaborate to create a chart outlining:
    - The problem.
    - Who is affected and how.
    - Their proposed solutions.
- Example scenario: *"Your local park is covered in litter. Families and children have stopped visiting. What can your group do to solve this?"*
    - Expected solutions: Organizing a clean-up drive, creating posters to encourage people to dispose of waste responsibly.

3. Presentation and Reflection (15 Minutes)

Objective: Share insights and connect learning to real life.

Step 1: Group Presentations (10 Minutes)

- Each group presents their chart.
- Allow other groups to ask questions or offer additional ideas.

Step 2: Class Reflection (5 Minutes)

- Facilitate a discussion using prompts like:

  - "What did you learn from solving these problems?"

  - "Can you think of a time when you practiced civic responsibility?"

  - "How can we, as a class, take steps to improve our community?"

4. Conclusion (5 Minutes)

Objective: Reinforce key takeaways.

1. **Summarize the lesson:**

   - Define community and civic responsibility.

   - Emphasize the importance of small, consistent actions in making a difference.

2. **Assign a follow-up task:**

   - "Think of one action you can take this week to help your community. Write about it in your journal and share it in the next class."

Assessment:

- Evaluate group charts for understanding and creativity.

- Observe participation during group work and presentations.

- Assess the follow-up journal task to check individual engagement and reflection.

Notes for Teachers:

- Keep the atmosphere supportive to encourage all students to share ideas.

- Use examples from your local community to make the lesson relatable.

- Encourage creativity but guide discussions to ensure focus on civic responsibility.

English

Lesson Plan for Teaching an English Chapter Using Experiential Learning:

Topic: Character Analysis of the Protagonist

Target Audience: High School Students (Grade 10)

Duration: 60 Minutes

Objective:

By the end of the lesson, students will be able to:

1. Understand the protagonist's traits, motivations, and development.

2. Relate the protagonist's experiences to real-life scenarios.

3. Develop analytical skills by discussing the character with their peers.

Materials Required:

- Copies of the selected English chapter or story.

- Sticky notes and markers.

- Chart paper for group activities.

- Audio-visual aids (short clips or images related to the story).

Lesson Flow

1. Introduction (10 Minutes)

1. **Start with a relatable scenario:**

   - Narrate a brief story from real life, such as a neighbor who overcame challenges to achieve a goal.

- Ask: *"Have you ever faced a situation where you had to make a tough choice? What did you do?"*

2. **Connect to the protagonist:**

- Introduce the protagonist and the challenges they face in the chapter.

- Briefly explain why understanding their character is important.

2. Experiential Activity: Walk in the Character's Shoes (30 Minutes)

1. **Step 1: Scene Reenactment (10 Minutes):**

- Divide students into small groups (4-5 members each).

- Assign each group a pivotal scene involving the protagonist.

- Ask them to act out the scene using their own words and style.

- Encourage them to think about how the protagonist feels and reacts in that situation.

2. **Step 2: Group Discussion (10 Minutes):**

- After the reenactments, each group discusses:

  - Why did the protagonist act in that way?

  - What could have been done differently?

- How does the scene relate to a situation they have seen or experienced in real life?

3. **Step 3: Reflection and Connection (10 Minutes):**

   - Ask each group to share their insights with the class.

   - Write key traits of the protagonist on the board (e.g., courageous, hesitant, kind, etc.).

   - Encourage students to reflect on whether they possess any of these traits and share examples.

3. Consolidation (15 Minutes)

1. **Chart Your Character:**

   - Provide chart paper and ask each group to create a "Character Map" for the protagonist.

   - Include:

     - Strengths and weaknesses.

     - Key decisions made by the character.

     - Lessons they learned.

2. **Present and Share:**

   - Groups present their character maps to the class.

   - Discuss how the protagonist's traits influenced the story's outcome.

4. Wrap-Up and Real-Life Connection (5 Minutes)

1. **Personal Application:**

   - Ask students to write a short note (2-3 sentences) on one trait of the protagonist they admire and how they can apply it in their own lives.

   - Example: "I admire the protagonist's courage. I will try to show courage by speaking up for what is right in my group projects."

2. **Homework:**

   - Assign a journal entry: *Write about a personal experience where you faced a challenge similar to the protagonist. How did you handle it, and what did you learn?*

Teacher's Role

- Facilitate discussions by asking probing questions like:

  - "What does this scene reveal about the protagonist's values?"

  - "Can you think of a real-life example that mirrors this situation?"

- Provide feedback on reenactments and group activities to encourage deeper thinking.

Expected Outcome

Students will develop a deeper understanding of the protagonist's character and learn to relate literature to their own lives. This will enhance their critical thinking and empathy.

By using experiential methods, students actively engage with the text, making the learning process meaningful and memorable.

Mathematics

Lesson Plan: Teaching the Concept of "Linear Equations in Two Variables" through Experiential Learning

Grade: High School (Grade 9 or 10)

Duration: 60 Minutes

Topic: Linear Equations in Two Variables

Objective

- To help students understand the concept of linear equations in two variables.

- To enable students to relate mathematical concepts to real-life situations.

- To encourage teamwork, critical thinking, and problem-solving through hands-on activities.

Materials Required

- Graph papers
- Markers or colored pencils
- Measuring tapes or rulers
- A simple budget chart (prepared beforehand)
- Whiteboard and markers

Lesson Flow

1. Introduction (10 Minutes):

Objective: Set the stage by connecting the topic to a real-life scenario.

1. Begin by asking the class:

   - "Have you ever calculated your expenses when planning for something, like a birthday party?"

   - "How do you balance between what you want to buy and the total money available?"

2. Show a simple budget scenario on the board:

   - E.g., "John has ₹500. He wants to buy pencils and erasers. Pencils cost ₹10 each, and erasers cost ₹5 each. How many of each can he buy?"

3. Explain that such problems can be modeled using linear equations with two variables (in this case, pencils and erasers).

2. Explanation (15 Minutes)

Objective: Teach the mathematical concept using clear and relatable examples.

1. Write a general form of the linear equation in two variables:

2. $ax+by=cax + by = cax+by=c$

   - Define xxx and yyy as variables, aaa and bbb as coefficients, and ccc as the constant.

3. Solve John's problem step by step:

   - Let xxx = the number of pencils and yyy = the number of erasers.

   - The equation becomes: $10x+5y=50010x + 5y = 50010x+5y=500$.

4. Discuss different possible combinations of xxx and yyy (e.g., if $x=20x = 20x=20$, $y=20y = 20y=20$).

5. Explain how plotting these points on a graph will show the relationship visually.

3. Experiential Activity (25 Minutes)

Objective: Apply the concept in a hands-on activity to strengthen understanding.

1. **Form Teams:** Divide students into small groups of 4-5 members each.

2. **Distribute Materials:** Provide each group with graph paper, markers, and a scenario sheet (a simple real-life situation similar to John's).

    Example Scenario:

    "A family is planning to buy apples and oranges for a party. Apples cost ₹30 per kg, and oranges cost ₹20 per kg. The budget is ₹600. How many kgs of apples and oranges can they buy?"

3. **Group Task:**

    - Model the situation as a linear equation in two variables.

    - List possible solutions (combinations of apples and oranges).

    - Plot the solutions on graph paper to visualize the equation.

4. **Discussion:**

- Ask each group to present their findings.

- Highlight how the graph represents all possible combinations within the given budget.

4. Wrap-Up and Reflection (10 Minutes)

Objective: Reinforce learning and connect back to real life.

1. **Summarize the key points:**

- What linear equations in two variables are.

- How they relate to real-life decision-making scenarios.

- How graphs help us visualize relationships between two variables.

2. **Reflection Questions:**

- "How did the activity help you understand the topic better?"

- "Can you think of other real-life situations where we might use such equations?"

3. **Homework Assignment:**

- Create a similar real-life scenario, form a linear equation for it, and solve it graphically.

Teaching Notes

- Use simple and engaging language during the lesson.

- Encourage students to ask questions and share observations during the activity.

- Walk around the room to provide guidance as needed.

By incorporating experiential learning, students not only understand the concept but also see its relevance in daily life, making mathematics more engaging and meaningful.

Science

Lesson Plan for High School Science Class (60 minutes)

Topic: Photosynthesis

Teaching Method: Experiential Learning:

Objective:

By the end of the lesson, students will:

1. Understand the process of photosynthesis.

2. Explain the role of sunlight, water, and carbon dioxide in the production of oxygen and glucose.

3. Relate photosynthesis to daily life, particularly its role in maintaining the balance of oxygen and carbon dioxide in the environment.

Preparation:

Materials Needed:

- Fresh green leaves (one per student group).
- Small, clear plastic bags.
- Rubber bands.
- Flashlights.
- Glass jars with water.
- A flip chart or board for visual aids.
- Handouts with diagrams of photosynthesis.

Lesson Outline:

1. Introduction (10 minutes)

Start with a Question:

- Ask, "Have you ever wondered how plants make their food? Can plants survive without sunlight?"

Connect to Daily Life:

- Mention a simple observation: "When you walk through a park, have you noticed the cool shade of trees? That's where life begins for us — plants produce the oxygen we breathe."

Set the Context:

- Briefly explain that plants use sunlight, water, and carbon dioxide to create food, a process called photosynthesis.

2. Experiential Activity (30 minutes)

Step 1: Group Formation (5 minutes)

- Divide the class into small groups of 5-6 students.

Step 2: Leaf Experiment (20 minutes)

Activity:

1. **Preparation:** Each group gets a green leaf and a clear plastic bag.

2. **Action:** Students wrap the leaf with the plastic bag and seal it using a rubber band, leaving the leaf attached to the plant.

3. **Observation:** They shine a flashlight on the leaf or keep it under sunlight for 10-15 minutes.

Guide Observations:

- Ask students to observe water droplets forming inside the plastic bag.

Discussion:

- Explain that the water droplets are a result of transpiration, which occurs alongside photosynthesis. Plants release oxygen and water vapor during this process.

Step 3: Demonstration with a Jar (5 minutes)

- Place a green plant cutting into a jar filled with water. Cover the jar with a transparent lid and expose it to light.

- Ask students to predict what they might observe over time (bubbles forming on the plant).

3. Explanation and Connection (15 minutes)

Discussion Questions:

1. "Why do you think plants need sunlight, water, and carbon dioxide?"

2. "How does this process benefit humans and animals?"

Diagram Explanation:

- Use the handout to explain the photosynthesis equation:

- $6CO2+6H2O+Light{\rightarrow}C6H12O6+6O26CO\_2 + 6H\_2O + Light \rightarrow C\_6H\_\{12\}O\_6 + 6O\_26CO2+6H2O+Light{\rightarrow}C6H12O6+6O2$

- Relate each part of the equation to what they observed in the activities.

Real-Life Connection:

- Highlight how photosynthesis produces oxygen, crucial for breathing.

- Discuss how plants serve as the foundation of food chains, providing energy for all living beings.

4. Recap and Reflection (5 minutes)

Recap:

- Summarize the experiment and key points about photosynthesis.

Reflection Questions:

- "What did you learn from today's activity?"

- "Can you think of ways to care for plants in your environment?"

Assessment:

- Each group presents their observations from the experiment.

- As homework, students write a short reflection on why photosynthesis is vital for life on Earth.

Conclusion:

End with a thought-provoking statement:

"Next time you take a deep breath, remember to thank the trees and plants around you. They work tirelessly to keep life on Earth going."

CONCLUSION

*"If we teach today's students as we taught yesterday's,
we rob them of tomorrow."*

– John Dewey

In today's fast-paced world, the role of teachers is more vital than ever. As educators, we hold a unique power to ignite curiosity and foster a love for lifelong learning in our students. By adopting experiential learning, we can convert traditional classrooms into engaging, interactive spaces where students actively participate in their own educational journey (Kolb, 1984). This call to action is for teachers to be ready to embrace this transformation and truly empower their students.

Embrace Curiosity in the Classroom

One way to make learning more impactful is to foster curiosity. Curiosity is a powerful driver that, when nurtured, can inspire students to delve deeper into subjects. Here's how:

1. **Ask Open-Ended Questions:** Encourage students to think more broadly and critically by asking open-ended questions that provoke thought. For example, instead of the straightforward "What is photosynthesis?" Consider asking "How might plants produce their food?" This reframing invites students to explore and think creatively (Mills & Treagust, 2003).

2. **Promote a Growth Mindset:** Cultivate a learning environment where mistakes are embraced as valuable learning opportunities. When students understand that errors are part of growth, they are more likely to approach challenges with resilience (Dweck, 2006).

3. **Encourage Innovative Thinking:** Present real-world problems and invite students to brainstorm novel solutions. This can help develop their problem-solving abilities while teaching them to think creatively about the challenges they encounter (Robinson, 2011).

Design Experiences that Are Both Meaningful and Relevant

For learning to be genuinely engaging, it needs to feel relevant and connected to students' lives. Here are ways to design impactful experiences in the classroom:

1. **Connect Lessons to Real-World Issues:** Ground lessons in real-world issues to make them relatable. For example, while discussing climate change, a field trip to observe the impact of pollution firsthand can turn an abstract topic into a concrete experience (Smith & Sobel, 2010).

2. **Incorporate Hands-On Activities:** Include hands-on activities such as experiments, role-playing, or simulations. These activities bring subjects to life, making learning memorable and meaningful for students (Bruner, 1960).

3. **Create Authentic Learning Opportunities:** Give students a chance to apply their knowledge in real-world situations, such as community service projects

or internships. This approach enables them to see the relevance of their learning and gain practical experience (Dewey, 1938).

Encourage Collaboration in Learning

Learning should be a collective process, where students feel connected and supported by their peers. Collaborative learning can help create this sense of community:

1. **Promote Group Work:** By participating in group activities, students learn teamwork and how to effectively collaborate, which builds essential interpersonal skills (Johnson & Johnson, 1994).

2. **Encourage Peer Feedback:** Set up a classroom environment where constructive peer feedback is normal. Students benefit from learning to give and receive feedback, a vital skill in personal and professional contexts (Hattie & Timperley, 2007).

3. **Build a Classroom Community:** Foster a community in which everyone feels valued and respected. A supportive classroom helps students thrive emotionally and academically, making them more open to learning (Putnam, 2000).

Reflect and Assess for Lasting Learning

Reflection is key for students to consolidate what they've learned. Regular reflection deepens understanding and helps students evaluate their progress:

1. **Encourage Journaling:** Let students document their learning experiences in journals. This reflective practice encourages them to think critically about what they've learned (Moon, 2006).

2. **Teach Self-Assessment Skills:** Help students develop the ability to evaluate their work. Providing clear learning objectives and rubrics empowers students to assess their own progress (Sadler, 1989).

3. **Use Formative Assessment:** Employ formative assessment techniques like quizzes, polls, or exit tickets to gauge understanding and provide feedback that supports student growth (Black & Wiliam, 1998).

Commit to Ongoing Learning

For educators, learning is a continuous journey. Staying curious and engaged with educational advances enables teachers to bring the best practices into their classrooms:

1. **Attend Educational Workshops:** Keep up with trends by participating in conferences and workshops focused on the latest methods in education (Guskey, 2000).

2. **Connect with Fellow Educators:** Networking with other teachers provides valuable insights, allowing for the exchange of ideas and resources (Darling-Hammond, 1998).

3. **Experiment with New Techniques:** Be open to trying innovative strategies and approaches. Experimentation can help teachers find what works best for their students (Brophy, 1998).

B. Transforming Education Through Experiential Learning

The potential of experiential learning to transform education is enormous. By embedding hands-on, real-world experiences in our curricula, we can enhance student engagement and equip them with critical skills that will prepare them for the future (Kolb & Kolb, 2005).

How Experiential Learning Benefits Students

Experiential learning offers several key benefits for students:

1. **Boosts Engagement:** Engaging students through hands-on activities helps capture their attention, leading to a more immersive learning experience (Csikszentmihalyi, 1990).

2. **Develops Critical Thinking Skills:** Experiential learning challenges students to analyze, evaluate, and synthesize information, promoting a higher level of cognitive engagement (Ennis, 1985).

3. **Strengthens Problem-Solving Abilities:** Through real-world projects, students learn to identify problems, gather information, and devise creative solutions (Jonassen, 2000).

4. **Encourages Creativity and Innovation:** By allowing students to explore unique approaches to problem-solving, experiential learning fosters creativity and innovation (Sternberg, 2003).

5. **Promotes Lifelong Learning:** When students are actively engaged, they are more likely to develop a

love of learning that lasts a lifetime (Falk & Dierking, 2000).

6. **Prepares Students for the Workforce:** Experiential learning helps students build practical skills essential for success in today's job market (Trilling & Fadel, 2009).

Strategies for Advocating Experiential Learning in Schools

Realizing the full benefits of experiential learning requires commitment from educators, administrators, and policymakers alike. Here are some specific steps we can take:

1. **Advocate for Experiential Learning:** It is essential to communicate the value of experiential learning to key stakeholders like school administrators, policymakers, and parents (Kolb & Kolb, 2005).

2. **Forge Community Partnerships:** Collaborate with local businesses, organizations, and institutions to create authentic learning opportunities for students (McLennan, 2008).

3. **Leverage Technology for Learning:** Incorporate digital tools like virtual field trips and online simulations to enhance experiential learning in the classroom (Prensky, 2001).

4. **Invest in Professional Development for Teachers:** Provide teachers with regular opportunities for professional development focused on experiential learning strategies (Darling-Hammond & Richardson, 2009).

5. **Focus on Student-Centered Learning:** Place students at the heart of the learning process, empowering them to take an active role in their own education (Felder & Brent, 1996).

By embracing these strategies and encouraging experiential learning, we can shape an educational landscape where students are equipped with the knowledge, skills, and confidence needed to thrive in a rapidly changing world. Teachers have the power to make learning meaningful and memorable, creating a legacy that extends far beyond the classroom.

Key Chapter Takeaways

- **The Power of Curiosity:** Fostering curiosity through open-ended questions, growth mindset, and innovative thinking can significantly enhance student engagement and learning.

- **Real-World Relevance:** Connecting lessons to real-world issues, incorporating hands-on activities, and creating authentic learning opportunities make learning more meaningful and impactful.

- **Collaborative Learning:** Promoting group work, peer feedback, and a supportive classroom community can enhance student learning and social skills.

- **Reflective Learning:** Encouraging journaling, self-assessment, and formative assessment helps students consolidate their learning and track their progress.

- **Lifelong Learning for Educators:** Teachers should stay updated through workshops, networking, and experimentation to continuously improve their teaching practices.

- **Benefits of Experiential Learning:** Experiential learning boosts engagement, develops critical thinking, strengthens problem-solving, encourages creativity, promotes lifelong learning, and prepares students for the workforce.

- **Advocating for Experiential Learning:** Advocating for experiential learning, forging community partnerships, leveraging technology, investing in professional development, and focusing on student-centered learning are crucial steps to implement experiential learning effectively.

- **The Role of Teachers:** Teachers play a pivotal role in igniting curiosity, fostering a love for learning, and empowering students through experiential learning.

- **Transforming Education:** By embracing experiential learning, we can transform traditional classrooms into engaging, interactive spaces where students actively participate in their own education.

- **The Future of Education:** Experiential learning equips students with the necessary skills to thrive in a rapidly changing world, making it a crucial component of modern education.

ENDNOTES

*This section contains a detailed list of notes, references, and citations for each chapter of this book. I hope most readers will find this list sufficient. However, I understand that scientific literature evolves over time, and some references may need to be updated. If you notice any errors, such as incorrect attribution of an idea or a missed acknowledgment, please feel free to email me at **authorpkroy@gmail.com** so I can correct it promptly.*

Introduction

1. Gentry, J.W. (1990). *What is experiential learning? Guide to Business Experiential Learning,* 1(2), 9-17.

2. Itin, C.M. (1999). Reasserting the philosophy of experiential education as a vehicle for change in the 21st century. *The Journal of Experiential Education,* 22(2), 91–98.

3. Kolb, D.A. (2015). *Experiential learning: Experience as the source of learning and development* (2nd ed.). Pearson Education.

4. Kraft, R.J., & Kielsmeier, J.C. (1995). Experiential learning and social change: Learning through experience. Retrieved from https://www.ericdigests. org/1997-2/learning.htm

5. Smith, M.K. (2016). *David A. Kolb on experiential learning. The Encyclopedia of Pedagogy and Informal*

Education. Retrieved from https://infed.org/mobi/david-a-kolb-on-experiential-learning/

Chapter-1

1. Beard, C., & Wilson, J.P. (2013). *Experiential learning: A handbook for education, training and coaching.* Kogan Page Publishers.

2. Dewey, J. (1938). *Experience and education.* Kappa Delta Pi.

3. Hedin, N. (2010). *Experiential learning: Theory and challenges*, in D. Houle, R. Gibralter, & S. Whealon (Eds.), *Learning through experience.* Wiley.

4. Itin, C.M. (1999). Reasserting the philosophy of experiential education as a vehicle for change in the 21st century. *Journal of Experiential Education*, 22(2), 91-98.

5. Kolb, D.A. (1984). *Experiential learning: Experience as the source of learning and development.* Prentice-Hall.

6. Kolb, D.A., Boyatzis, R.E., & Mainemelis, C. (2001). Experiential learning theory: Previous research and new directions, in R. J. Sternberg & L. Zhang (Eds.), *Perspectives on cognitive learning, and thinking styles* (pp. 227-247). Routledge.

7. Lewin, K. (1946). Action research and minority problems. *Journal of Social Issues*, 2(4), 34-46.

8.   Smith, L. (2001). Learning through doing: The art and science of experiential learning. *Educational Journal*, 24(3), 45-50.

Chapter-2

1.   Beard, C., & Wilson, J.P. (2013). *Experiential Learning: A Handbook for Education, Training and Coaching.* Philadelphia, PA: Kogan Page.

2.   Dewey, J. (1938). *Experience and Education.* New York: Macmillan.

3.   Gentry, J.W. (1990). What is experiential learning? *Guide to Business Experiential Learning*, 1(2), 9-17.

4.   Hedin, N. (2010). Experiential learning: Theory and challenges. *Christian Education Journal*, 7(1), 107-117. https://doi.org/10.1177/073989131000700108

5.   Itin, C.M. (1999). Reasserting the philosophy of experiential education as a vehicle for change in the 21st century. *The Journal of Experiential Education*, 22(2), 91–98. https://doi.org/10.1177/105382599902200206

6.   Kolb, D.A. (1984). *Experiential learning: Experience as the source of learning and development.* Englewood Cliffs, NJ: Prentice-Hall.

7.   Kolb, D.A. (2015). *Experiential learning: Experience as the source of learning and development* (2nd ed.). Pearson Education.

8.   Kolb, D.A., Boyatzis, R.E., & Mainemelis, C. (2001). Experiential learning theory: Previous research and

new directions, in *Perspectives on Thinking, Learning, and Cognitive Styles*. Mahwah, NJ: Lawrence Erlbaum Associates.

9. Kraft, R J., & Kielsmeier, J.C. (1995). *Experiential learning and social change: Learning through experience.* Retrieved from https://www.ericdigests.org/1997-2/learning.htm

10. Lewin, K. (1946). Action research and minority problems. *Journal of Social Issues*, 2(4), 34-46. https://doi.org/10.1111/j.1540-4560.1946.tb02295.x

11. Schön, D.A. (1983). *The Reflective Practitioner: How Professionals Think in Action.* Basic Books.

12. Smith, M.K. (2001). David A. Kolb on experiential learning. *The Encyclopedia of Informal Education.* Retrieved from http://infed.org/mobi/david-a-kolb-on-experiential-learning/

13. Smith, M.K. (2016). David A. Kolb on experiential learning. *The Encyclopedia of Pedagogy and Informal Education.* Retrieved from https://infed.org/mobi/david-a-kolb-on-experiential-learning/

Chapter-3

1. Gentry, M. (1990). *Creating a School-Wide Recycling Program.* Educational Leadership.

2. Kolb, D.A., Boyatzis, R.E., & Mainemelis, C. (2001). *Experiential Learning Theory: Previous Research and New Directions,* in *Perspectives on Thinking, Learning,*

and Cognitive Styles (pp. 227-247). Lawrence Erlbaum Associates.

3. Schön, D A. (1983). *The Reflective Practitioner: How Professionals Think in Action.* Basic Books.

Chapter-4

1. Beard, C., & Wilson, J.P. (2013). *Experiential Learning: A Best Practice Handbook for Educators and Trainers.* Kogan Page.

2. Gentry, J.W. (1990). What is experiential learning?, in J. W. Gentry (Ed.), *Guide to Business Gaming and Experiential Learning* (pp. 9-20). Nicholas Brealey Publishing.

3. Hedin, D. (2010). Experiential learning: The importance of an active approach. *Journal of Experiential Education*, 33(2), 113-129.

4. Itin, C. (1999). Reasserting the philosophy of experiential education as a vehicle for change in the 21st century. *Journal of Experiential Education*, 22(2), 91-98.

5. Kolb, D.A. (1984). *Experiential Learning: Experience as the Source of Learning and Development.* Prentice Hall.

6. Kraft, R.J., & Kielsmeier, J. (1995). Service-learning: A practical guide to the principles and practices. *The Service-Learning Directory*, 1-23.

7.   Schön, D.A. (1983). *The Reflective Practitioner: How Professionals Think in Action*. Basic Books.

8.   Smith, M.K. (2001). David A. Kolb on experiential learning. *The Encyclopedia of Informal Education*. Retrieved from http://infed.org/kolb_experiential_learning.shtml

Chapter-5

1.   Bransford, J.D., Brown, A. L., & Cocking, R. R. (2000). *How people learn: Brain, mind, experience, and school*. National Academy Press.

2.   Craft, A. (2005). Creativity in schools: Tensions and dilemmas. *Routledge*.

3.   Davis, M.H. (1994). Empathy: A social psychological approach. *Westview Press*.

4.   Dewey, J. (1938). *Experience and education*. Kappa Delta Pi.

5.   Facione, P.A. (2011). *Critical thinking: What it is and why it counts*. Measured Reasons.

6.   Garmston, R.J., & Wellman, B.M. (2016). *The adaptive school: A sourcebook for developing collaborative groups*. Rowman & Littlefield.

7.   Goleman, D. (1995). *Emotional intelligence: Why it can matter more than IQ*. Bantam Books.

8.   Johnson, D.W., & Johnson, R.T. (2014). *Joining together: Group theory and group skills*. Pearson.

9. Kolb, D.A. (1984). *Experiential learning: Experience as the source of learning and development.* Prentice Hall.

10. Partnership for 21st Century Skills. (2009). *Framework for 21st century learning.* Retrieved from http://www.p21.org/our-work/p21-framework

11. Robinson, K. (2011). *Out of our minds: Learning to be creative.* Capstone.

12. Sawyer, R.K. (2012). *Explaining creativity: The science of human innovation.* Oxford University Press.

13. Trilling, B., & Fadel, C. (2009). *21st-Century skills: Learning for life in our times.* Jossey-Bass.

Chapter-6

1. Billig, S.H. (2000). *Service-learning and civic engagement.* Phi Delta Kappan, 81(9), 658-664.

2. Bringle, R.G., & Hatcher, J. A. (1996). *Implementing service learning in higher education.* Journal of Higher Education, 67(2), 221-239.

3. Dewey, J. (1938). *Experience and education.* Macmillan.

4. Eyler, J., & Giles, D. E. (1999). *Where's the learning in service-learning?* Jossey-Bass.

5. Hamilton, M.A., & Hamilton, S.F. (1997). *When is learning work-based? Findings from a study of work-based learning programs for youth.* Journal of Vocational Education Research, 22(4), 259-284.

6. Jacoby, B. (2015). *Service-learning essentials: Questions, answers, and lessons learned*. John Wiley & Sons.

7. Kolb, D.A. (2015). *Experiential learning: Experience as the source of learning and development*. Pearson Education.

Chapter-7

1. Bergmann, J., & Sams, A. (2012). *Flip your classroom: Reach every student in every class every day*. International Society for Technology in Education.

2. Darling-Hammond, L. (2006). *Powerful teacher education: Lessons from exemplary programs*. Jossey-Bass.

3. Dewey, J. (1938). *Experience and education*. Kappa Delta Pi.

4. Freire, P. (1970). *Pedagogy of the oppressed*. Continuum.

5. Kolb, D.A. (1984). *Experiential learning: Experience as the source of learning and development*. Prentice-Hall.

6. Wiggins, G., & McTighe, J. (2005). *Understanding by design*. Association for Supervision and Curriculum Development (ASCD).

Chapter-8

1. Barrett, H.C. (2000). *Create your own electronic portfolio*. Learning & Leading with Technology, 27(7), 14-21.

2. Barrows, H.S., & Tamblyn, R. M. (1980). *Problem-based learning: An approach to medical education*. Springer.

3. Beane, J.A. (1997). *Curriculum integration: Designing the core of democratic education*. Teachers College Press.

4. Bredderman, T. (1982). *What research says: Activity science–The evidence shows it matters*. Science and Children, 20(1), 39-41.

5. Darling-Hammond, L. (2006). *Powerful teacher education: Lessons from exemplary programs*. Jossey-Bass.

6. Dewey, J. (1938). *Experience and education*. Kappa Delta Pi.

7. Epstein, J.L. (2001). *School, family, and community partnerships: Preparing educators and improving schools*. Westview Press.

8. Fullan, M. (1993). *Change forces: Probing the depths of educational reform*. Falmer Press.

9. Pantelidis, V.S. (2009). *Reasons to use virtual reality in education and training courses and a model to determine when to use virtual reality*. Themes in Science and Technology Education, 2(1-2), 59-70.

10. Papastergiou, M. (2009). *Exploring the potential of computer and video games for health and physical education: A literature review.* Computers & Education, 53(3), 603-622.

11. Thomas, J.W. (2000). *A review of research on project-based learning.* Autodesk Foundation.

12. Toshalis, E., & Nakkula, M.J. (2012). *Motivation, engagement, and student voice.* Jobs for the Future.

Chapter-9

1. Andrade, H.L. (2000). Using rubrics to promote thinking and learning. *Educational Leadership, 57*(5), 13-18.

2. Black, P., & Wiliam, D. (1998). Inside the black box: Raising standards through classroom assessment. *Phi Delta Kappan, 80*(2), 139-148.

3. Boud, D. (1995). Enhancing learning through self-assessment. Routledge.

4. Boud, D., Keogh, R., & Walker, D. (1985). Reflection: Turning experience into learning. Kogan Page.

5. Danielson, C. (2007). Enhancing professional practice: A framework for teaching. ASCD.

6. Flick, U. (2018). An introduction to qualitative research. SAGE Publications.

7. Hattie, J., & Timperley, H. (2007). The power of feedback. *Review of Educational Research, 77*(1), 81-112.

8. Kolb, D.A. (1984). Experiential learning: Experience as the source of learning and development. Prentice-Hall.

9. Paulson, F.L., Paulson, P.R., & Meyer, C.A. (1991). What makes a portfolio a portfolio? *Educational Leadership, 48*(5), 60-63.

10. Topping, K. (1998). Peer assessment between students in colleges and universities. *Review of Educational Research, 68*(3), 249-276.

11. Trilling, B., & Fadel, C. (2009). 21st-century skills: Learning for life in our times. John Wiley & Sons.

Chapter-10

1. Dweck, C.S. (2006). *Mindset: The new psychology of success.* Random House.

2. Fullan, M. (2007). *The new meaning of educational change* (4th ed.). Teachers College Press.

3. Grant, S. (2014). *Personalized project-based learning for the 21st century student.* ISTE.

4. Guskey, T.R. (2000). *Evaluating professional development.* Corwin Press.

5. Hattie, J. (2015). *Visible learning for teachers: Maximizing impact on learning.* Routledge.

6. Higgins, L., Hall, E., Wall, K.,

Conclusion

1. Black, P., & Wiliam, D. (1998). Assessment and classroom learning. *Assessment in Education: Principles, Policy & Practice, 5*(1), 7–74.

2. Bruner, J.S. (1960). *The process of education.* Harvard University Press.

3. Brophy, J.E. (1998). *Motivating students to learn.* McGraw-Hill.

4. Csikszentmihalyi, M. (1990). *Flow: The psychology of optimal experience.* Harper & Row.

5. Darling-Hammond, L. (1998). Teachers and teaching: Testing policy hypotheses from a national commission report. *Educational Researcher, 27*(1), 5–15.

6. Darling-Hammond, L., & Richardson, N. (2009). Teacher learning: What matters? *Educational Leadership, 66*(5), 46–53.

7. Dewey, J. (1938). *Experience and education.* Kappa Delta Pi.

8. Dweck, C.S. (2006). *Mindset: The new psychology of success.* Random House.

9. Ennis, R.H. (1985). A logical basis for measuring critical thinking skills. *Educational Leadership, 43*(2), 44–48.

10. Falk, J.H., & Dierking, L. D. (2000). *Learning from museums: Visitor experiences and the making of meaning.* AltaMira Press.

11. Felder, R.M., & Brent, R. (1996). Navigating the bumpy road to student-centered instruction. *College Teaching, 44*(2), 43–47.

12. Guskey, T.R. (2000). *Evaluating professional development.* Corwin Press.

13. Hattie, J., & Timperley, H. (2007). The power of feedback. *Review of Educational Research, 77*(1), 81–112.

MAY I ASK YOU A LITTLE FAVOR?

First and foremost, I would like to express my sincere gratitude to you for taking the time to read my book. With so many other options available, the fact that you chose to read it, means a great deal to me. I genuinely hope that you find a few valuable takeaways that can assist you in your daily endeavors.

If you don't mind, I would like to request an additional 30 seconds of your time. It would be greatly appreciated if you could leave a review of the book. Positive reviews can encourage others to give my work a chance, ultimately expanding my readership. Thank you for your consideration.

DIRECT REVIEW LINK FOR
"Master the Art of Experiential Learning"

Email: authorpkroy@gmail.com

Please write your review; it will only take a minute of your time, but it will significantly help me in reaching out to more people.

I appreciate your encouragement regarding my efforts and eagerly anticipate reading your review.

A SPECIAL GIFT FOR YOU!

I want to offer you a gift as a token of my gratitude for taking the time to read this book. This gift is a 20-page PDF action guide titled *How to Be the Teacher Students Never Forget*. It's concise enough to skim quickly, yet packed with actionable advice that can truly enhance your life as a teacher.

You can get immediate access to *How to Be the Teacher Students Never Forget* by clicking the link below and joining my mailing list.

Download Your Free Gift

https://p-k-roy.ck.page/873d4b9039

You might wonder how valuable a free gift can be. But I believe you'll be pleasantly surprised. This guide is filled with practical tips and strategies that you can start using right away to make a real difference in your teaching.

Don't just take my word for it—join tens of thousands of other readers and see for yourself. I'm confident that you will find ***How to Be the Teacher Students Never Forget*** to be immediately helpful.

Dr. P.K. Roy

Write to us at: **authorpkroy@gmail.com**

ACKNOWLEDGMENTS

I extend my heartfelt gratitude to everyone who played a significant role in the publication of my book, *Master the Art of Experiential Learning.*

First and foremost, I extend my heartfelt gratitude to Dr. Cyriac Thomas for graciously writing the foreword for my book, *Master the Art of Experiential Learning.* As a distinguished academician and former Vice-Chancellor of Mahatma Gandhi University, Kottayam, his insights and deep understanding of education add immense value to this work. His lifelong dedication to fostering quality education, from his early days as a lecturer at St. Thomas College, Pala, to his esteemed role as a Member of the National Commission for Minority Educational Institutions of India, is truly inspiring. Thank you, Dr. Cyriac Thomas, for your thoughtful words and unwavering commitment to the field of education.

I express my sincere thanks to Dr. Prof. George Kareckat for his unwavering support, encouragement, and guidance throughout this journey.

I am deeply appreciative of my editors—Mr. Charles Smith, Mr. Dayanand E., Mrs. Jozina Braggs, Dr. Lizy Sunny Stephen, and Mrs. Jaimol John —whose meticulous attention to detail and invaluable insights elevated this manuscript to its present form.

I am profoundly indebted to my superiors, well-wishers, and friends, whose unwavering support and encouragement inspired me to see this project through to completion.

A special note of gratitude goes to my mentor, Mr. Som Bathla, and the dedicated team at Notion Press. Their steadfast support and expertise were instrumental in bringing this book to life and ensuring its message reaches readers across the globe.

I am also deeply thankful to all the readers of my previous books who took the time to write to me, sharing their love and kindness.

To all who contributed to this endeavor, your efforts have been a source of strength and inspiration. Thank you.

This book is part of the *'Educator Thought'* Series designed specifically for teachers.

You can explore the other books in the series below.

Master the Art of Teaching

&

Master the Art of Cooperative Learning

Order Your Copies of the Book Today

Master the Art of Teaching

https://notionpress.com/in/read/master-the-art-of-teaching

Master the Art of Cooperative Learning

https://notionpress.com/in/read/master-the-art-of-cooperative-learning